Praise for *Rewire Your Mind*

"This might be the single most important mindfulness book I've ever read. Why? Because we all want to be happier. We all want to love ourselves more. But very few books tell you exactly how to do it. Shauna has created a roadmap. The perfect mix of science, stories, practices, and wisdom with one goal: to help you love yourself and your life—even when things get messy. Run (don't walk!) toward this book and read it now. Read it with your whole heart. The practices will change your life."

JUSTIN MICHAEL WILLIAMS
author of *Stay Woke*

"A beautifully written, inspiring, yet highly practical book on how to cultivate mindfulness and self-compassion. Equal parts wisdom, science, and personal story, it will surely transform the lives of those who read it."

KRISTIN NEFF, PHD
co-author of *The Mindful Self-Compassion Workbook*

"Shauna Shapiro offers us the gift of a well-proven path to peace and joy in our lives."

DANIEL GOLEMAN
author of *Emotional Intelligence*

"Dr. Shapiro is one of the most thoughtful, dedicated, and articulate scientists in the field of mindfulness and compassion. Drawing on her decades of personal practice and research, she has written a practical manual that can help you attain greater clarity, calm, and joy."

ANDREW WEIL, MD
author of *Spontaneous Happiness* and *Eight Weeks to Optimum Health*

"A lovely invitation to live with mindfulness and compassion. Dr. Shapiro brings together practical training, neuroscience research and a big heart to show the path to a wise, loving, and gracious way of being."

JACK KORNFIELD
author of *A Path with Heart*

"A beautiful and wise book that opens the path of love and understanding through realizing mindfulness in our everyday lives."

REV. JOAN JIKO HALIFAX
author and abbot, Upaya Zen Center

"Shauna Shapiro reminds us that self-compassion is essential for our healing and freedom and offers a lucid, loving, and wise guide for navigating the path."

TARA BRACH, PHD
author of *Radical Acceptance* and *Radical Compassion*

"The perfect combination of inspiration, science, heart, and practical tools. From a world-class authority on mindfulness and compassion, this book is simply brilliant. Reading it feels like a dear wise friend greeting you with the words of its title!"

RICK HANSON, PHD
New York Times bestselling author of *Buddha's Brain: The Practical Neuroscience of Happiness, Love, and Wisdom*

"In this exhilarating and moving synthesis of clinical experience, science, story, and practice, Shauna Shapiro will take you on a journey to acceptance and joy. It is an absolutely fresh and insightful take on mindfulness and its many extensions. It will change how you look at the world and how you feel about your life."

DACHER KELTNER, PHD
founder and faculty director at The Greater Good Science Center at UC Berkeley and author of *Born to Be Good* and *The Power Paradox*

"Dr. Shapiro is one of the most thoughtful, eloquent, and dedicated scientists in the field of mindfulness and compassion. Her decades of personal practice combined with scientific study make this book a true gem."

CHIP CONLEY
hospitality entrepreneur and bestselling author of *Wisdom at Work*

"Long a leading advocate and practitioner of meditation, Dr. Shauna Shapiro gives us an indispensable guide to mindfulness, through the portals of curiosity, kindness, and compassion toward self and, inevitably, toward others. A beautiful book."

GABOR MATÉ, MD
author of *In the Realm of Hungry Ghosts: Close Encounters with Addiction*

"Shauna Shapiro's simple yet profound practices encourage us to hold ourselves—our whole selves—with love and kindness. I'm deeply touched by her work." **EILEEN FISHER** founder and co-CEO of EILEEN FISHER, Inc.

"Shauna combines decades of personal meditation practice with years of rigorous scientific study, making her specially qualified to bring the miracle of mindfulness alive for you through this simple yet powerful book." **SHINZEN YOUNG** author of *The Science of Enlightenment*

"What a tour de force! This is one of the most engaging and powerful books I've read on how to lead our best lives. Impressive, important, and profound." **JAMES R. DOTY, MD** founder and director, Center for Compassion and Altruism Research and Education, Stanford University School of Medicine, and *New York Times* bestselling author of *Into the Magic Shop*

"Radically transformative—a beam of bright light in the darkness. Highly recommended!" **DEAN ORNISH, MD, AND ANNE ORNISH** *New York Times* bestselling authors of *Undo It!*

"Mindfulness expert and professor Dr. Shauna Shapiro makes a compelling case for how we can thrive personally and succeed professionally not by beating ourselves up, but instead by extending compassion toward ourselves. Deeply insightful, rich in practical instruction, and backed by cutting-edge science, this book will transform your life."

MIRANDA MACPHERSON spiritual teacher and author of *The Way of Grace*

"Shauna Shapiro has written an excellent book! Filled with personal stories and compelling neuroscience research explains in an engaging, user-friendly style how mindfulness and self-compassion work and why they're so good for you. Highly recommended!"

JAMES BARAZ co-author of *Awakening Joy: 10 Steps That Will Put You on the Road to Real Happiness* and co-founder of Spirit Rock Meditation Center

"Her depth of personal practice and commitment to clear and accessible mindfulness instructions compel us all to follow Dr. Shapiro as our trusted guide in the roadmap of transformation she deftly provides in this book." *AMISHI JHA, PHD*
neuroscientist and researcher

"The one book on mindfulness you must read. A deeply wise, fresh, and brilliant guide to how mindfulness and self-compassion can help heal ourselves and our world." *KRISTINE CARLSON*
co-author of the bestselling *Don't Sweat the Small Stuff* books

"In an age of anxiety, we need new manuals for addressing the fractures in our psyche. Dr. Shapiro weaves together decades of scientific study, personal stories, and powerful practices to fill our minds and hearts with actionable insights."

JASON SILVA
filmmaker, futurist

"So many of us chide ourselves for not being more perfect or mistakenly believe that self-judgment will help us improve, make us better. Dr. Shapiro busts this whole mindset. Her pioneering work in mindfulness offers us both the science and practice of how self-kindness is the secret sauce of fulfillment, transformation, and joy."

LORIN ROCHE
author of *The Radiance Sutras*

"A deeply wise yet practical manual on how mindfulness and self-compassion can heal us and the world. Dr. Shapiro's writing provides readers with the science behind why our inner criticism exacerbates our suffering, as well as the practical means for developing our capacity for self-compassion in order to ease this suffering. Her clarity and wisdom shine through in this beautiful work, from which we can all benefit." *MARK COLEMAN*
author of *From Suffering to Peace*

"What would you get if you took a brilliant academic who had done two decades of pioneering research and dedicated personal practice of meditation and asked her to distill the wisdom she had gleaned into her most helpful gift to the world? Well, you would get this beautiful, wise, loving book offering us ways to live with greater contentment, compassion, and joy."

ROGER WALSH MD, PHD, DHL
University of California Medical School, author of *Essential Spirituality: The Seven Central Practices to Awaken Heart and Mind*

"The singular insight that mindfulness flourishes when we attend with curiosity and kindness drives this personally compelling account and tethers it to cutting-edge science. What a gift to those in search of greater presence and ease."

ZINDEL SEGAL, PHD
author of *Mindfulness-Based Cognitive Therapy for Depression*

"A wise, approachable, yet practical book of how mindfulness and self-compassion can increase your happiness and transform your life."

SONJA LYUBOMIRSKY
distinguished professor of psychology, University of California, Riverside, and author of *The How of Happiness*

"What a perfect way to jumpstart or restart your mindfulness journey. Carry this book with you and gift it to those who need it."

WALLACE J. NICHOLS, PHD
marine biologist and author of *Blue Mind*

"Shauna Shapiro combines the rigor of science, the beauty of art, and the wisdom of practice in this informative and deeply inspiring book."

SCOTT SCHUTTE
senior vice president, LinkedIn

REWIRE YOUR MIND

REWIRE YOUR MIND

Discover the Science + Practice of Mindfulness

SHAUNA SHAPIRO PHD

An Hachette UK Company
www.hachette.co.uk

The authorized representative in the EEA is Hachette Ireland,
8 Castlecourt Centre, Dublin 15, D15 XTP3, Ireland (email: info@hbgi.ie)

First published in Great Britain in 2020 by Aster, an imprint of
Octopus Publishing Group Ltd
Carmelite House
50 Victoria Embankment
London EC4Y 0DZ
www.octopusbooks.co.uk

First published in United States as *Good Morning, I Love You* in 2020
by Sounds True, Boulder, CO 80306

ISBN 978 1 78325 293 0

Printed and bound in UK

10 9 8 7 6 5 4 3

All reasonable care has been taken in the preparation of this book but the information it
contains is not intended to take the place of treatment by a qualified medical practitioner.

Before making any changes in your health regime, always consult a doctor. While all
the practices detailed in this book are completely safe if done correctly, you must seek
professional advice if you are in any doubt about any medical condition. Any application of
the ideas and information contained in this book is at the reader's sole discretion and risk.

> *For my parents, Deane and Johanna*

Wherever you are is the entry point.

KABIR

Contents

Foreword by Daniel J. Siegel, MD

author of the *New York Times* bestseller
Aware: The Science and Practice of Presence

If you are interested in learning simple and profound steps to achieving more clarity and calm in your life, this wise and accessible guidebook offers the science-supported ideas and practices that have been demonstrated to bring mental well-being into our lives. If you are also interested in learning how to create a more compassionate, kind, and loving way of being in this world—being more positive in your inner life and within your relationships—then here you'll find just that: the direct, no-nonsense, research-informed ways to bring a more rewarding approach to living every day. In addition, if you take in the suggestions from our expert guide, Shauna Shapiro, PhD, you'll also be building the focused attention and intention, the open awareness, and kind, compassionate attitude that Shapiro herself has been a major scientific contributor in demonstrating bringing health into our lives.

Research from Dr. Shapiro and a host of other dedicated researchers over the last two decades has demonstrated that the accessible mind training steps you'll be offered in this book can bring a wide range of changes to your body and its brain. Among these research-established outcomes are reduced levels of the stress hormone, cortisol; enhanced immune and cardiovascular functions; decreases in inflammation; and optimization of an enzyme, telomerase, that maintains and repairs the important ends of your chromosomes to keep your cells, and you, healthy, and even slows down aging!

In brain studies, these practices that build attention, open awareness, and cultivate an attitude and intention of kind regard and compassion, have been shown to lead to changes in the brain's structure. As Shapiro's message reveals, "What you practice grows stronger" is the aphorism for the science of neuro-plasticity—how the brain changes in response to experience. The neuroplastic changes emerge from a process that can be summarized as this: where attention goes, neural firing flows, and neural connection grows. This book will teach you how to focus your attention to activate networks in your brain in a specific manner that will change their structure. No kidding. How you focus your mind can change the physical structure of your brain!

What are these changes in brain function and structure that arise from the practices you are about to learn? These can be summarized with one word, "integration." Integration here means the linking of differentiated parts. In the brain, this means, for example, how the left and right sides of the brain are more connected with the growth of the interconnecting fibers known as the corpus callosum. Integration is also revealed in the growth of the linking networks known as the prefrontal cortex and hippocampus. And, as if these important brain integrative regions were not enough, research has also demonstrated that the "connectome"—the connections among the widely separated and differentiated areas of the brain—will become more interconnected. Yes, that's how it is said. A more "interconnected connectome" is how you'll be achieving more integration by reading this book and trying out its simple yet powerful practices.

All of this means that you'll literally be able to grow a more integrated brain. Why would this matter for you? Name a kind of process and its regulation, and you'll find in the research literature that they all depend on integration. These might include emotion and mood, thought and reasoning, morality and relational behavior, empathy and compassion, and even attention and consciousness itself. These various aspects of "self-regulation" help us not only achieve more balance in life, but they are the foundation for well-being of mind and body. With simple, regular practice, we create a focused, kind, and open state of mind. With repeated practice, that powerful state can become a trait. Where attention goes, neural connection grows: what we practice grows stronger.

Shauna Shapiro has played an important role in the research on how to cultivate more empathy in medical students, how to conceptualize mindfulness in our lives, and how self-compassion plays a role in being more mindful. She has been pivotal in helping us see that the excitement about mindfulness in our culture, in education, in our clinical practice, and in our scientific research is more than just its power to sharpen our attention and hone our thinking; mindfulness also includes a kind attitude that imbues life with a loving quality that heals the heart, brings warmth to our relationships, and brings resilience into our approach to the world. Beyond this important role in science that she has played, our guide comes to mindfulness from a personal experience of medical challenges that made learning to open her awareness with kindness through extensive in-depth training a pivotal moment in her own development.

I have known Professor Shapiro for over a dozen years, teaching with her in a range of settings locally and abroad, and have seen firsthand how inspiring her offerings have been to a wide range of participants in workshops and attendees of public and professional conferences. This book is a wonderful distillation of her powerful scientific, educational, and personal journey into cultivating more well-being in our lives. Reading these pages has been a joy. I've learned a lot, cried and laughed, and felt fuller and freer from these wise words. I hope you will too! Welcome to a wonderful journey into bringing more kindness and love into your life, inside and out.

Daniel J. Siegel, MD
Executive Director, Mindsight Institute
Clinical Professor, UCLA School of Medicine

PART 1

What You Practice Grows Stronger

1

A MONK'S WHISPER

What you practice grows stronger.

a British monk I met in Thailand

It is never too late to rewire your brain and transform your life. I know this is possible for you because I experienced it. The practices contained in this book offer a roadmap for strengthening the brain's circuitry of deep calm, contentment, and clarity. Best of all, you can begin wherever you are. As the fifteenth-century Indian poet Kabir says, "Wherever you are *is* the entry point."

My entry point came at my lowest moment: I was seventeen, lying in a hospital bed, a metal rod in my spine, watching my life as I knew it dissolve before my eyes.

I seemed to be living the dream in beautiful Laguna Beach, California. I'd been crowned homecoming princess, had led our volleyball team to win a state championship, and had just received early admission to Duke University to play volleyball on their NCAA volleyball team.

A few months before graduation I was sitting on the examining table in my orthopedic surgeon's office, waiting for him to come in and do the routine checkup I'd had countless times to monitor my scoliosis. I'd had this spine curvature since birth, but it hadn't interfered with my life. My doctor and I had forged a close relationship, and I was eager to tell him about the volleyball championship and Duke.

I vaulted off the table the moment the door opened—but the look on my doctor's face stopped me short.

"Shauna, the X-rays show that your scoliosis has gotten worse. The bones in your spine are going to puncture your lungs unless we do something. We need to operate."

I was stunned, whiplashed by his words. And then: a rising tide of terror.

The weeks before the surgery were an eternity in purgatory. I was haunted by the image of that large metal rod going into my spine. My mind was locked into a future of dread and despair.

When I woke after the operation, I went from purgatory to hell: I was in excruciating pain and could barely move. I realized that my life as I knew it—and my future as I had dreamt it—were gone.

Throughout months of rehabilitation, I struggled to live in a stranger's body, and worse still, a stranger's mind. Gone was the spunky, athletic teen. In her place was a meek, frightened little girl. Every movement was awkward and painful.

But my mind tortured me most. I lay there, feeling ever more hopeless and terrified: *Will I always be in pain? I'm never going to play volleyball again. No one at college will like me. Who will ever love me? No one will be attracted to this broken body with huge, red scars.*

I tried to push through it. I forced myself to think positive thoughts, but they couldn't quell the tremendous fear and pain within. I tried distracting myself with visits from friends and by watching movies, but nothing quieted the worries raging in my head.

Then hope arrived from a place I least expected. Although my father and I shared a deep love, we were often at odds and fought about almost everything.

Our relationship changed after my surgery. I'll never forget the day he walked into my room, eyes filled with fatherly love and concern, and handed me a book. It was a copy of *Wherever You Go, There You Are* by Jon Kabat-Zinn, a pioneer in the field of mindfulness.

I gasped as I read the opening paragraph: "Whatever has happened to you, it has already happened. The important question is, how are you going to handle it?"[1]

I read on, often through tears, as this wise book revealed a possibility that had eluded me for months: *I could be happy again.* My resilience, shrouded by months of fear and pain, began to waken. I felt a flicker of hope—hope that I could heal.

I read every book, article, and essay on mindfulness that I could find. The more I read and practiced, the more I began to notice small changes. Instead of dwelling on the past or obsessing about the future, I started to discover little moments of peace in the present.

These little moments—the in-between moments—began to matter: when my mom opened the window and the smell of ocean air enveloped me, when the last ray of sunlight retreated for the night. I even heard magic as my dad played his silver flute, which only a few months earlier had routinely embarrassed me in front of my friends.

As my mind settled, the pain in my body began to shift. My relationship to the sensations was different. It was no longer "my pain"; rather, it became "the pain." And when I didn't exacerbate things with my fears, I began to notice moments of peace. Although the pain remained, I suffered less.

My progress was gradual, sometimes almost imperceptible, but I felt each improvement acutely. Every tiny gain motivated me to keep going.

My mom still tears up when she recounts the moment, four months after surgery, when she knew I would be okay. I was home, still in a hospital bed, but my scars were healing well, and I was finally walking without help.

On a whim, I announced I was going to the beach for a swim. I shed the frumpy grey sweatsuit that had been my uniform and donned my favorite blue swimsuit. Mom watched my emaciated body gingerly navigating the shifting sands as I made my way toward the water. She remembers holding her breath as my fire-engine red scars eased into the brisk whitewash of waves.

In the moment after the water washed over my head, just before I emerged to open my eyes, I felt a spark of life flash through me. A sense of rebirth and the strength to begin again. In that moment, somehow, my mom and I both knew I was going to be okay.

That swim was the start of a metamorphosis. Even though my daily progress was still barely visible, my faith, joy, and hope were restored. I knew that despite everything that had happened, and whatever might happen, there was something inside me that was indestructible. My journey had begun.

Flash forward four years: I'm riding on a rickety motorcycle through sticky tropical heat, arms in a death grip around my friend Robyn's waist as we careen down a winding gravel road with near-zero visibility. It is our third day in Thailand. We're looking for a temple hidden under a waterfall.

I had met Robyn at Duke, where we were both enrolled in Dr. Craighead's infamous 8:00 am Abnormal Psych course. I was a diligent freshman and she was a "cool" sophomore, but we were kindred spirits and formed what would become a life-long friendship through conversations about psychology, boys, and the meaning of life.

During my final year at Duke, Robyn called me from London, where she was working. She was planning a trek to Nepal and Thailand and wanted me to join.

Join my best friend on an adventure where I could continue my study of mindfulness, in a place where it had been practiced for centuries? I shouted an enthusiastic "yes!"

Despite the sweat stinging our eyes as we zoomed down the road, Robyn somehow spotted the tiny wooden sign marking the trail to the waterfall monastery.

Swatting away bugs and hacking our way through the lush jungle in our outfits of sarongs and flip-flops wasn't easy, but finally we saw it: the sun illuminating iridescent water cascading down a roaring waterfall. That meant the monastery lay just ahead.

We scrambled down slippery, moss-covered stone stairs. At the bottom stood a monk in saffron robes. Without a hint of surprise at our arrival, he welcomed us and invited us to meditate with him. As we tiptoed into the humble stone building, the scent of incense enveloped us. Formidable, vine-covered walls enclosed a modest altar with a small Buddha statue and a single burning candle, surrounded by an assortment of meditation cushions.

My mind raced. *Omigod, this is the real thing: a real monk, a real temple, real meditation cushions!* Then the meditation session began.

To this day, I can feel how my body and breath expanded the moment I closed my eyes. Time disappeared as a quilt of ease, clarity, and calm swaddled my mind. And then something astonishing happened. For the first time since my surgery nearly four years earlier, I felt complete comfort in my body. No pain. No fear. The boundaries of my body dissolved. I felt connected to everything with an absolute sense of peace.

The bell rang, signaling the end of the session. I looked over at Robyn. She held up her watch and mouthed, "It's been an hour!" It had felt like an instant.

As I left the temple, still wrapped in bliss, the monk looked into my eyes and whispered two simple but potent words: "Keep practicing."

One week later, on the strength of the monk's whisper, I walked through the gates of a Thai monastery to begin my first meditation retreat. The monks didn't speak much English, and I didn't speak any Thai, but I knew mindfulness was about being present, and after my experience at the waterfall monastery, I felt confident and excited to begin.

The first morning, we gathered in the large meditation hall overlooking a beautiful pond filled with lotus flowers. I couldn't imagine a more perfect setting for beginning my first retreat.

The initial instructions, given in rudimentary English, were simple and straightforward: feel the breath going in and out of my nose. I began. One breath. Two breaths. My mind wandered off. I brought it back. One breath. Darn! It wandered again.

Until now, much of my study of mindfulness had been theoretical. The real thing was proving far different from what I had imagined. I'd expected meditation to be similar to the peaceful and healing experience I'd had at the waterfall temple. Yet here I was, struggling just to keep my mind present. It was sucked into the past: *If only I had_____. I wish I hadn't_____.* Or it vaulted into the future: *What if_____? How will I ever _____? What will I do when_____?*

The more I tried to force my mind to be still, the more my attention darted from one thought to another. I finally understood the meaning of "monkey mind," a term I'd often seen in mindfulness readings to describe how our mind swings from thought to thought like a monkey swinging from limb to limb. My hopes for having the "perfect" meditation retreat in this "perfect" setting came crashing down.

Given the language barrier, and the fact that it was a silent retreat, I was unable to talk to the monks about my struggles. Left to my own devices, I dove into an abyss of self-judgment: *What is wrong with you? You are terrible at this. Why are you even here? You think you're so spiritual. You're a fake.*

Worse still, I started judging everyone around me, even the monks: *Why are they just sitting here? Shouldn't they be doing something?*

Fortunately, an English-speaking monk from London arrived the next day and I was granted a meeting with him. When I shared how hard I was trying, and how terribly my mindfulness practice was going, he responded with a heartfelt chuckle: "Oh, dear, you're not practicing mindfulness. You're practicing judgment, impatience, and frustration."

Then he said five words that I will never forget: "What you practice grows stronger."

This monk grasped bedrock truths about the brain that neuroscientists were just beginning to discover at the time: whatever we practice moment by moment physically alters our brain. *What we practice grows stronger.*

The monk went on to explain that if we practice mindfulness with judgment, we are growing judgment. If we practice with frustration, we are growing frustration. He taught me that mindfulness isn't just about paying attention. It's about *how* we pay attention.

> *Mindfulness isn't just about paying attention. It's about **how** we pay attention.*

True mindfulness involves an attitude of kindness and curiosity. This wise monk explained that the practice of mindfulness was like feeling the loving embrace of a dear friend, welcoming all of our experience. Even the messy, imperfect parts.

What I only glimpsed at that time—but became the focus of my research and my life's work—is that cultivating an attitude of kindness and compassion is the "secret sauce" of mindfulness.

To be clear, this attitude of kindness isn't about letting ourselves off the hook or papering over difficult things. Instead, it's a way to become truly accountable for all of our emotions, thoughts, and actions. We learn to understand and heal rather than blame and shame.

In short, I now understood that *how* we pay attention—our *attitude*—was as important as our **attention** itself.

But there's a third element of mindfulness I had yet to learn. Toward the end of the week, the monk pointed out that we are practicing something all the time—not just when we're meditating, but in every moment. This means we are growing something all the time.

So, the most important question becomes: What do you want to grow? This is your **intention**: what you care most about—your personal values, goals, and aspirations.

> *We are practicing something all the time—not just when we're meditating, but in every moment. This means we are growing something all the time. So the most important question becomes: What do you want to grow?*

Gradually, with the monk's help, my practice shifted. I began to observe my judgmental voice, instead of believing it. I stopped trying to control my experiences, instead approaching them with curiosity, interest, and kindness. I began to relax a bit more into my experience, instead of trying to "do it right." I realized that mindfulness practice was exactly that: it was about *practice, not perfection*.

As I said goodbye to the monastery and began my journey home, I felt deeply happy. Not the ephemeral happiness based on external events, but rather a deep sense of contentment arising from shifts in my internal landscape. Only later would I learn that researchers were proving in the lab what I had discovered in the monastery: *External* changes will not make us happier long-term, but *internal* changes can.

In Search of the Science— and a New Model of Mindfulness

I returned to the US determined to understand what I had experienced and share it with others. After graduating from Duke, I spent the ensuing six years studying the science behind mindfulness, focusing on the importance of incorporating *intention* and *attitude* to the practice.

Over twenty years of clinical work and scientific study, I've witnessed the positive effects of mindfulness and compassion practices on thousands of people—from hard-driving CEOs to stressed-out college students, from overwhelmed new mothers to women with breast cancer, from anxious young children to military veterans with PTSD to patients in palliative care.

Although the field continues to evolve with new research and insights, there are two key findings that we see again and again:

1. *The practice of mindfulness works.* It's good for you. It strengthens immune function, reduces stress, improves sleep, and offers countless other benefits to you and your family, workplace, and community.

2. *Having the right attitude and intention is essential.* Kindness and curiosity serve as basic building blocks for meaningful and lasting change.

This second finding is often overlooked, yet it's essential to unlocking the full power of our mindfulness practice. In my work with people from all walks of life, I have found one surprising constant: irrespective of our economic, educational, social, or personal circumstances, all of us struggle with self-judgment and self-criticism—an underlying sense of "I'm not good enough."

Worse still, when we see our shortcomings or have made a mistake, we tend to beat ourselves up, thinking this will help us improve. But self-flagellation is entirely counterproductive. Not only does it feel awful, research shows that shame doesn't help us learn new behaviors and change. Shame cannot work, because it shuts down the centers of the brain responsible for learning and growth.

> *Shame cannot work, because it shuts down the centers of the brain responsible for learning and growth.*

In contrast, the attitudes of kindness and curiosity release a cascade of chemicals that turn on the learning centers of our brain, giving us the resources we need for lasting transformation.

In 2000, my PhD advisor, professor Gary Schwartz, and I published a new paradigm for mindfulness.[2] It was the first scientifically based model that explicitly included intention, attention, and attitude—the key elements of mindfulness that I'd discovered in Thailand:

1. *Intention* directs the compass of our heart, reflecting our deepest hopes and values.

2. *Attention* trains and stabilizes our mind in the present moment.

3. *Attitude* refers to how we pay attention— with an attitude of kindness and curiosity.

As I continued to research mindfulness, the monk's words kept echoing in my ears: *What you practice grows stronger.* As we'll explore in the next chapter, neuroscience is catching up with ancient wisdom. Discoveries about the brain's lifelong ability to change and grow have revealed that we can, indeed, strengthen and rewire the brain through practice.

We can even rewire our brain to become happier.

Until recently, psychologists and researchers believed that our happiness levels didn't change much over our lifetime, always returning to a baseline level no matter what happened to us. For example, research found that people who win the lottery have an initial surge in happiness, but within a year return to their baseline level. Even more surprising, people who are paralyzed for life in a devastating accident have an initial plummet in happiness, but within one year they, too, return to their baseline levels.[3]

This *happiness setpoint theory* suggested that our happiness baseline is determined primarily by heredity and personality traits ingrained early in life and that this baseline cannot be changed.

But our brains are much more plastic than we thought. Although we're not all born equally happy, we can all become happier. Revolutionary findings in neuroscience have demonstrated that we can change our happiness setpoint. But it's not through changing our external life. It's through changing our internal landscape.

Although I didn't yet understand the science behind it, I had experienced this at the monastery in Thailand. My recent experiences of happiness and peace were due to internal changes in my ways of perceiving, experiencing, and relating to life, not to any external changes that had occurred.

The take-home: *External* changes (such as winning the lottery) won't shift our baseline happiness, but *internal* changes can. "Happiness can be trained because the very structure of our brain can be modified," says neuroscientist Richard Davidson.[4]

Training Your Brain for Happiness

Training your brain for happiness is the aim of this book.

In the chapters to come, we'll be weaving together ancient wisdom and scientific research to formulate the most potent practices for living a happy, meaningful life. You'll learn how to use mindfulness coupled with compassion not only for peace of mind in challenging times, but to add more depth and joy to everyday life.

This book will give you the keys to learning and growing in ways you may not have dared to hope. In my case, these practices led to a new perspective on life. I came to understand that my scoliosis and surgery, which I'd thought had shattered my dreams, had actually led me to a more enduring happiness than I'd ever known.

You will learn practices in each chapter that will help you in every aspect of your life—in your family, your relationships, your work, your health, and your pursuit of happiness.

Individually, these practices will help you sculpt neuropathways of clarity and kindness. Collectively, they will help us live in a more connected, compassionate world.

Perhaps best of all, you don't have to wait to begin. As Jon Kabat-Zinn reminded me in my darkest hour, we can start to practice right here, *right now*.

PRACTICE **Intention Practice**

It is essential to begin this book with an understanding of why you are reading it. *What are you hoping for?* This is where the power of intention comes in. Our intention sets the stage for what is possible, helping us stay connected with our personal blueprint for what we value most in life.

What are you hoping for? On some deep level, you already know the answer to this question. The practice below provides you with a space to let this knowledge rise to the surface so you can bring it with you as you read the chapters that follow and apply the practices to your life.

Begin by sitting quietly and allow your attention to rest on the natural flow of the breath rising and falling in the body. Feel yourself grounded and present. Invite in an intention for this journey.

Ask yourself: What truly motivates me at this time? What do I care about? In what direction do I want to set the compass of my heart?

For example: "May I find greater happiness." "May I become a more compassionate and wiser parent." "May I feel at peace in my life."

Tip: Don't make this a mental activity where you are striving to choose the "right" or most "perfect" intention. Simply listen, feel, and open yourself to whatever arises. Stay curious and kind.

When you are ready, allow your eyes to open, and write down your intention. If no clear intention came to you, simply set an intention to keep listening with kindness and curiosity.

I suggest you keep a journal (on paper or electronic) for this inner exploration and for the practices in later chapters.

———————————

GOLD NUGGET   Instead of a dry, textbookish summary, we will end each chapter with a *Gold Nugget*—the key teaching to take with you. According to Nobel prize-winning psychologist Daniel Kahneman, the "peak-end rule" teaches us that we remember the peak and the end of an experience. That's why I suggest reflecting on the "peaks" of the chapter, and choosing one peak most memorable to you to write down at the "end" of each chapter, to help reinforce the highlights and encode them in your long-term memory.

So please take a moment now and reflect on the key teachings in this chapter. Some Gold Nuggets might include:

- What you practice grows stronger
- Practice, not perfect
- Kindness matters
- Happiness is based on internal, not external factors

Once you've reflected on the highlights of this chapter, choose one Gold Nugget that speaks strongly to you and write it in your journal. By the end of the book, you will have collected eleven Gold Nuggets to bring with you into your life.

2

THE MIRACLE OF NEUROPLASTICITY

Habits are human nature.
Why not create some that will mint gold?

HAFIZ fourteenth-century Persian mystical poet,
in *The Subject Tonight Is Love*

While you are reading this, your brain is quietly overseeing a boggling array of tasks. It is governing the movements of your eyes as you scan down the page. It's decoding squiggles into words based on lessons begun in childhood, synthesizing them into meaning without conscious effort. Your neural pathways—connecting one part of the nervous system to another—are humming as you file ideas away in your memory so you can retain them days, weeks, months, even years after you have finished this book.

At the same time, your brain is making sure you remain alive: the lungs oxygenating the body via the breath, the heart pumping blood and carrying nutrients to your trillions of cells, the digestive system processing your last meal. You don't need to do anything to make all of this happen. You don't have to think about it, control it, or remember to do it. It is simply the miracle of life.

These are only a few of the nearly countless tasks your brain is performing—just in the last several seconds.

But there's more. As mentioned briefly in the previous chapter, revolutionary findings in neuroscience have shown that our brain development doesn't stop at a certain age, as previously believed. Our brain, far from being static or fixed in its potential, can change throughout our entire lifespan.

We now understand how the brain works, how it grows, and how we can purposefully shape it through practice. With every passing day we are literally training our minds and changing our brains, so we can flourish individually and collectively.

It's Never Too Late to Change Your Brain

The most important discovery in brain science of the twentieth century—*neuroplasticity*—has found that our brain is constantly changing throughout life. No matter how old you are, you can actually sculpt new healthy pathways in the brain and prune away old, unhealthy ones.

This discovery of neuroplasticity changed everything. Why? Because it confirms our boundless potential. It affirms our remarkable capacity to adapt and grow, not just when we're young, but *at any time*. In every moment of your life, you have the capacity to change the physical architecture of your brain. You can grow new neural connections, strengthen existing ones, and eliminate connections that are no longer useful. You can, quite literally, transform your mind.

If transformation is possible, why do so many of us remain stuck? As psychologist Tara Brach puts it, "Perhaps the biggest tragedy of our time is that freedom is possible, yet we pass our years trapped in the same old patterns."[1] We long to feel joy and ease, to take risks, to be authentic and open. Yet too often, fear and doubt hold us back. We fear we can't change our habits. We doubt it will make any difference. We persist in thinking "it's too late."

The science of neuroplasticity offers a radical new perspective. It proves that it's never too late to change, grow, learn, and develop. You have the choice and the power.

Now, this isn't like flipping a switch that instantly turns off the bad and lights up the good. Change requires commitment. It requires repeated practice. But each day offers infinite possibilities for practice. And with practice, each and every one of us is capable of transformation.

To begin, let's take a closer look at our miraculous brain.

Growing, Wiring, Pruning: The Cultivation of Our Marvelous Mind

Although it's impossible to measure precisely, scientists believe that our brains operate at the speed of one exaFLOP: one billion billion calculations per second, or one billion times faster than your computer. The brain alone comprises 1.1 trillion cells, including 100 billion neurons working together to govern different parts of our life, from eating and sleeping to laughing or falling in love. Inconceivable? Yes. Yet every one of us is carrying this amazing organ atop our shoulders.

You might say that our brain is like a perfect personal assistant. It knows what needs to be done and does it without our having to ask, performing the vast majority of tasks flawlessly. Still, for certain key activities of life, especially those that govern our happiness and satisfaction, we must provide training so our assistant knows what to do in order to achieve optimal results. We can consciously direct our brain by focusing on which neural pathways we want to grow and develop.

There's a well-known phrase among neuroscientists: *neurons that fire together wire together*. Every time neurons are activated and "fire" together, those neural connections grow stronger. This neurophysiological process—called cortical thickening—refers to the growth of new neurons and synaptic connections resulting from repeated practice. As we practice something—be it a physical activity or a thought pattern—the neurons associated with that activity become more connected, and the brain becomes stronger and actually changes.

For example, pioneering research in the field of neuroplasticity found that London taxi drivers have bigger and stronger areas of the brain responsible for visual-spatial mapping and memory. Why does this happen? To operate one of London's iconic black taxi cabs in the complex urban maze of twenty-five thousand streets, drivers must pass one of the most rigorous exams in the world, known simply as "the Knowledge." Drivers who pass the Knowledge study for an average of four years—that's as long as it takes to complete medical school in the US.

Researchers at University College London demonstrated that drivers who passed the Knowledge had measurable changes in their brains.[2] They concluded that those cabbies who repeatedly practiced navigating the twenty-five thousand streets of London all day, every day for years had grown, or thickened, the area of their brain related to visual-spatial mapping, known as the hippocampus.

Similarly, research by professor Sara Lazar and colleagues at Harvard used fMRI to look at the brains of people who practice mindfulness. They found that the areas of the brain related to attention, learning, and emotional processing were bigger and stronger.[3] Not only that, but the researchers concluded that mindfulness practice might slow the aging process of the brain: "Meditation practice may slow age-related thinning of the frontal cortex."

Bottom line: These findings support what the monk from Thailand so adeptly taught me more than twenty years ago: *What you practice grows stronger.*

What's more, while we're sculpting and strengthening positive synaptic connections—shaping our cerebral architecture in healthy ways—we're simultaneously ridding ourselves of unhealthy pathways. Scientists call this "neuronal pruning." When we do not practice certain thoughts, feelings, or behaviors, the brain does not "fire" the associated neurons. As a result, those thoughts, feelings, and behaviors grow weaker and eventually wither away. This is why you can't play the clarinet as you could back in high school, and it's also why you probably no longer remember how to calculate the area under a curve.

From an evolutionary standpoint, neuronal pruning is imperative. It means that we can intentionally strengthen certain connections while simultaneously pruning pathways that are no longer serving us. Pruning allows the brain to reserve space for the neurons we need most: the ones that will best support us in being happier, healthier, and more effective.

For example, I often need to practice patience. Each time I pause and take a breath before I react, I am both *growing* the neuronal pathway of patience and *pruning* pathways of impulsiveness and impatience. It's truly a win-win.

Superhighways of Habit Versus Country Roads of Compassion

I like to think of neuropathways as roads that can take us in any direction. We all have well-grooved superhighways of habits that we've practiced for decades. These might be automatic emotional reactions, like quickly losing one's temper. They might be ingrained belief systems, like believing you're not good enough. Or they might be willpower-quashing behaviors, like repeatedly hitting snooze and missing that morning workout.

As we become aware of these superhighways of habit, something important happens. *We put ourselves back in choice.* Each time we recognize that we're about to take one of these superhighways, we find ourselves at a choice point. These choice points give us the opportunity to consciously carve out a new neural pathway instead of mindlessly taking the same old route.

Think of these new pathways as country roads. The country roads are less traveled and initially not as fast. But they are the pathways of evolution, bringing us to new places and experiences. Superhighways of habit only lead to places we've been before. What happens when we want to go somewhere new?

If we keep using the same old superhighway, we'll end up in the same old spot, unable to find the new place we want to go for one simple reason: our superhighways don't go there. As the saying goes, insanity is doing the same thing over and over again and expecting different results.

To go somewhere new, we must carve out new country roads—practice new neural pathways. As we travel down these country roads more frequently—as we practice—they gradually become their own superhighways, replacing the old ones that now serve no purpose other than to delight the neural pruning demolition crews.

As an example, think about the last time you saw a baby crawl across the floor with the incredible speed of a Hot Wheels car. Then imagine this baby taking her first precarious steps, only to fall down, giggle, pop back up, and stumble on. Years later, this same baby can walk, run, skip, and dance without even thinking about the advanced motor skills required.

Change requires this dedication to practice, and importantly, as we'll discuss, the same lack of self-judgment that enables babies to go from crawling to walking to running despite their repeated wipeouts.

Fortunately, our brain is built to bootstrap itself forward, if we give it the chance. We can even train our mind just by *imagining* an action. Researchers at the National Institutes of Health conducted an experiment where half the subjects did five-finger piano exercises while the other half simply imagined doing the same exercises.[4] In the group that physically did the exercises, the part of the brain that controls finger motor skills grew larger. In the half that only imagined the exercises, the brain grew in the same way!

If we have this remarkable capability, why do so many of us repeatedly end up back on the superhighways of habit, giving up too quickly on the country roads, mistakenly believing they will never get us to our destination? Therein lies the problem: we focus on the destination—a static place where we've finally "made it." Yet this focus on a perfect end is not what life is about. The only time life ends is . . . well, you know.

Life itself is about process. It is always evolving. Perfection is a static state. It is the antithesis of evolution.

Many of our greatest minds understood this. Renowned painter Salvador Dali advised, "Have no fear of perfection, you'll never reach it." Philosopher Immanuel Kant noted, "Out of the crooked timber of humanity, no straight thing was ever made."

If these great icons understood that perfection is not possible, why do we continue to admonish ourselves for not being perfect? To transform our lives, we must liberate ourselves from the myth of perfection.

> To transform our lives, we must liberate
> ourselves from the myth of perfection.

American football legend Vince Lombardi proclaimed, "Perfection is not attainable, but if we chase perfection we can catch excellence." This famous coach knew that it was the *pursuit* that led to excellence. To transform our lives, we must focus on our direction, not our destination.

> To transform our lives, we must focus
> on our direction, not our destination.

Practice, Not Perfect

Consider the following questions:

- In rush hour traffic, can you remain perfectly calm?

- Can see your neighbors travel to fantastic places without a twinge of jealousy?

- Can you love everyone around you unconditionally?

- Can you always find contentment just where you are?

If you can answer yes to all four of these questions, then probably, you are . . .

A DOG.

I hope you are laughing right now or at least have a smile on your face—and maybe also are feeling a subtle sense of relief. Of course you can't live up to all of those idealistic standards. No human being can. And yet, as you were reflecting on the questions, if you are like me, perhaps you were judging yourself for not measuring up to them.

We hold ourselves to impossible standards of perfection, and then disparage ourselves when we don't live up to them. It seems that no matter how hard we try, no matter how successful we are—it's never enough.

So, what do we do? We try harder, work more, push, strive, and judge. Our efforts make the hamster wheel of life spin faster and faster. This pursuit of perfection leaves us feeling inadequate, exhausted, lonely, and besieged by a sense of deficiency.

Paradoxically, the harder we try to find happiness by living up to some ideal of perfection, the more elusive real peace, happiness, and connection become. We lose touch with what matters, with what is deepest in ourselves, which is the true source of peace and transformation. All we see is that we're not measuring up. Dispirited and defeated, we give up.

I remember one cold winter's day when it seemed the rain would never stop, and my mood seemed just as dreary. Wrapped in a shawl, I was sitting on my therapist's couch, recalling yet again some incident in which I had been reactive and impatient—not the calm and loving meditation teacher I'd hoped to be. "Why aren't I improving?" I asked him.

He looked at me and said, "Shauna, life is not a self-improvement project." I almost fell off the couch. I suddenly realized that my whole life had been focused on self-improvement: an endless quest for some future state of perfection where I would finally be loveable, and I could finally rest. Worse, I realized I was using my mindfulness practice as one more measuring stick that would inevitably show me falling short.

We must change our mind-set from one of *self-improvement* to one of *self-liberation*. Self-liberation means freedom from our limiting beliefs, our misguided idea that there is something wrong with us that needs to be "fixed." Our constant attempts to "get it right" and to be "perfect" leave us in a state of exhaustion, never resting in the present moment, never happy with who we are.

As we continue this journey together, take this to heart: The goal of practice is not to get it right once and for all. It's about practice, not perfect. ***Perfection isn't possible, but transformation is.*** One of my favorite Zen sayings embodies this paradox: "You're perfect as you are, and there is room for improvement."

> *Perfection isn't possible,*
> *but transformation is.*

Change, then, is a direction, not a destination. Our world is always changing, challenging us to change with it. That's why our brain was designed to constantly learn and develop through practice.

In fact, Angela Duckworth, bestselling author of *Grit*, has found that it's practice and perseverance, not innate talent, that predict success.[5] In everyone from Olympic athletes to West Point graduates to CEOs to violin virtuosos, the consistent differentiator between success and failure was not their level of talent, but their commitment to practice. And practice is within reach of everyone.

This more empowering mind-set requires that we reassess many of the "facts" about personal change that society has conditioned us to believe, such as the benefits of "no pain no gain" or "whipping ourselves into shape." In chapter 5 you'll learn the science behind why these popular notions are actually incorrect—and you will learn scientifically proven alternatives to replace them.

When we liberate ourselves from the notion of perfection and place our focus on our desired direction, we open up to an important fact: there are infinite possibilities in every moment.

We aren't changing ourselves so much as liberating our best self. This path is not a self-improvement project with perfection as its ever-receding goal. Instead, it's about opening to the possibility of change, growth, and evolution. As the brilliant psychiatrist Dan Siegel reminds us, "We are always in a perpetual state of being created and creating ourselves."[6]

The 5 Percent Principle

Now, if you're thinking this sounds like a lot to accomplish and you're feeling a little overwhelmed, don't worry. Change happens in small increments. We know this from experience: we can't instantly erase an unproductive habit and attain a behavior we want. Yet instead of seeing this as a normal process of change, we tend to punish ourselves each time we "fail."

Personal change is not linear. There are stops, detours, setbacks, serendipities, and surprises. Transformation is longitudinal and it is experiential. Layer upon layer, we literally integrate new ways of thinking, feeling, and behaving as we lay down new pathways in our brain and then let these pathways express themselves in our thoughts, words, and actions.

But for anything to happen, we have to start. Sometimes that's the hardest part.

The key is to develop "micro habits"—small shifts in behavior that lead to big changes. I often invite my clients to set "ridiculously *un*ambitious goals," a phrase I learned from my colleague,

Dr. Christine Carter, author of *The Sweet Spot*. Taking baby steps gives us permission to lighten up and take the pressure off. It purposefully primes us for success early and often. With each accomplishment, we become more motivated to achieve the next milestone. These little moments and little victories lead to momentous change.

Even the smallest experiences count, especially if repeated again and again. Consider drops of water dripping into a bucket. The first few drops don't seem like much, but eventually the bucket will overflow. When we struggle with an all-or-nothing mentality instead of embracing and celebrating small increments of change, we get so focused on the finish line that we're often less efficient at getting there. Research bears this out: people who break a complex task down into smaller milestones and then set about accomplishing them finish the task faster and with better quality than those who focus entirely on the end result.[7]

To help yourself stop worrying over the ultimate destination and focus instead on direction, try asking yourself, "Can I do just 5 percent?" So, for example: "Can I do 5 percent more exercise? Can I relax 5 percent more? Trust 5 percent more?" And if 5 percent feels like too much: "Can I do 1 percent?"

You might think a few degrees won't amount to much, but they do. I distinctly remember as a little girl having a fever, feeling shaky and achy, eyes watering, face flushed. My father pointed out that if we could just lower my temperature a degree or two from 101, I would feel infinitely better. He was right. Subtle is significant.

Every Moment Matters

I heard the following story from Buddhist teacher and author Jack Kornfield, who heard it from the great spiritual teacher Ram

Dass. I am not sure of its origins, but it beautifully illustrates how every moment, no matter how insignificant it may seem, influences how our brain grows, in turn dictating how our life goes, and even how we impact the lives of others:

> A young army lieutenant was referred to a mindfulness course to better manage his severe anger issues. He was initially reluctant, but his military-imbued sense of duty compelled him to begin the training in earnest, dedicating himself to the practices that he hoped would stem his somewhat frequent anger outbursts. After six weeks of practice, he shared this story:
>
> One Saturday he was waiting to check out at the bustling local supermarket. Already a bit sweaty from the sweltering heat wave that overpowered the market's air conditioning, he seethed with anger when he noticed that the woman in front of him was in the wrong line. She had only a single item and should have been one lane over in the express line, which was completely empty. The woman was carrying a baby boy, and before the checkout clerk rang up the single item, they both began cooing over the baby. The officer fumed to himself, "What is this, a nursery!?"
>
> Then to his dismay, the woman handed the little boy to the checkout clerk. The officer erupted inside, "What are you doing! There are three people behind you in line and you're not even supposed to be in this line in the first place!" But because he had been practicing mindfulness, he avoided going down the habitual highway of an anger outburst. Instead, he took some deep breaths, relaxed, and as the smoke of anger cleared, he was able to notice that the little boy was quite cute.

When he got to the young checkout clerk, he noted, "You know, that little boy was really cute." She looked up at him, eyes sparkling with delight, and said, "Oh, really? He's my son." Then her voice softened, becoming more somber, "My husband died in combat last year. So now I have to work full-time and I don't get much time with him. I'm lucky that my mom is here to take care of him. She brings him through my lane each day so I can give him a hug and tell him I love him."[8]

Can you feel how everything changed in that moment? Imagine how grateful he felt that his mindfulness practice had enabled him to notice his anger and manage it. In that little moment there was a big victory.

Positive Neuroplasticity

All of us have this capacity—the power to choose what we want to grow. This is why psychologist and author Rick Hanson coined the term *positive neuroplasticity*: intentionally engaging in practices that will hardwire constructive psychological resources into our brain.[9]

No matter where you are in life, no matter what pain you've experienced or mistakes you've made, your future is spotless, and you can begin again.

I know you can do it because of five simple words: *what you practice grows stronger*. The only question is: What do you want to grow?

PRACTICE What Do You Want to Grow?

The first step in any practice is to connect with your goals. What is important to you? What do you want to cultivate and grow?

Begin by sitting quietly and allowing your attention to rest on the natural flow of your breath, rising and falling in your body. Reflect on the saying we mentioned earlier: "You are perfect as you are, and there is room for improvement."

We all have something we want to get better at, something we want to grow. Something inside of you knows it is time to begin. That is why you are reading this book. Trust this part of yourself.

Gently ask yourself: *What do I want to grow?*

Tip: Listen to whatever responses arise. Stay open, kind, and curious. For example: "I want to become better at managing stress in my life, especially over the small things." "I want to be kinder to myself." "I want to become a more attuned and attentive parent/spouse/friend."

As a clear idea arises, if it feels good in your body—if there's a sense of *ahhh, yes*—then you know you've found your intention for what you want to grow. It could be a sentence, a phrase, an image, or just a word. Whatever it is, when it comes to you, it will feel like it clicks into focus and becomes definitive and compelling.

When you are ready, write down your intention.

PRACTICE **Gentle Reminders**

Now that you have your intention for what you want to grow, set a daily calendar reminder for first thing in the morning to remind you of your intention. Be on the lookout for at least one choice point in your day where you can remember your intention.

Recall that choice points are those moments when we could either blindly veer onto the superhighway of habit or purposefully venture down the country road toward where we truly want to go.

Each day, write down your intention, the choice point, and which path you chose.

———————————

GOLD NUGGET Pause and reflect on the highlights from this chapter and then choose one Gold Nugget you want to take with you and encode in your long-term memory. Write it down in your journal.

Sample Gold Nuggets:

- Perfection isn't possible, but transformation is.
- Take small steps, make 5 percent shifts.
- Every moment matters.
- It's never too late to change your brain.

3

MINDFULNESS

Seeing Clearly

The true voyage of discovery is not in seeking
new landscapes but in having new eyes.
MARCEL PROUST *Remembrance of Things Past*, vol. 5

Jose, a twenty-nine-year-old gang member, was my first patient at the Tucson Veteran's Hospital. He was referred to work with me because he was suffering from ongoing panic attacks, which began shortly after a rival gang tried to kill him.

When Jose arrived in my office and saw a twenty-six-year-old white woman sitting in the "therapist" chair, he rolled his eyes.

"Look," he said quickly, "I just want some medication to get rid of these feelings in my body."

"I'm sorry," I said, "I have a PhD, not an MD, so I cannot prescribe medication."

He frowned and shrugged: "Fine—just teach me how to distract myself so I don't have to feel this way."

"Actually, I'm a mindfulness therapist, so instead of distraction techniques, you and I will work together to bring our attention to the anxiety in your body, so we can start to heal it."

"You're going to make me focus even more on this?" he nearly shouted. And then under his breath, "Sh*t . . . I want a new therapist."

I took a steadying breath. "Jose, let me ask you a question. If the gang members who tried to kill you were walking behind you on the street, would you want the chance to turn around and see them clearly—maybe see how many there were, what weapons they had—so you could decide how to respond? Or would you want to just ignore them and then get ambushed? What I'm asking you to do here with your anxiety is to learn how to see it clearly, so it doesn't keep ambushing you."

Jose's eyes met mine, and I knew we had begun. But what happened next, as you will see at the end of this chapter, surprised even me.

Mindfulness

When I decided to focus my research on mindfulness, I was told it would ruin my academic career. Many of my professors said I should choose something less "out there." In the twenty years since then, *Time* has featured "The Mindful Revolution" on its cover, the study and practice of mindfulness have blossomed, and mindfulness has found its way into nearly every facet of our society.

More than seven hundred hospitals, clinics, and medical centers now integrate mindfulness into their care, and mindfulness-based interventions are routinely covered by insurance. Fortune 500 companies such as Google, Facebook, General Mills, Procter & Gamble, and Cisco Systems offer mindfulness training to their employees. And universities such as Harvard, Yale, and Stanford all offer mindfulness courses as part of their curriculum.

As today's children deal with more stress and distraction than ever before, mindfulness is making its way into elementary and high schools, with pioneering programs such as Mindful Kids and Mindful Schools. In 2015 my colleagues and I published a review article demonstrating the beneficial effects of such training in schools, which helps students' mental and emotional health while increasing creativity, focus, and test scores.[1]

Mindfulness has even found its way into the military. The Department of Defense has invested several million dollars to study its applications. Research shows that mindfulness practice reduces symptoms of post-traumatic stress and helps soldiers make wiser choices during high-stress situations.

Although research has demonstrated the myriad benefits of mindfulness, the recent interest has often led to its oversimplification and over-commodification. The danger is that mindfulness can quickly turn into a caricature of itself that loses its transformational power. This watered-down version of mindfulness limits its full potential and can lead to discouragement and abandoning the practice as "not for me."

This book, in contrast, offers a comprehensive and clear understanding of mindfulness that will allow you to harness its radical power to rewire your brain and improve your life, using practices that you can easily incorporate into your daily routine.

So, What Is Mindfulness, Really?

The word "mindfulness"—*Sampajañña* in Pali—means clear comprehension. Mindfulness helps us to see clearly so we can make wise choices and respond to life effectively.

But seeing clearly is difficult because the lens through which we view the world is blurred by distorted ways of thinking. Our understanding of reality is formed by how we perceive each moment.

Often our perceptions are inaccurate, conditioned through past life experiences as opposed to present-moment reality.

Our parents, teachers, relationships, and society at large all influence our perceptions on conscious and subconscious levels. Our well-meaning parents may tell us, "Life is dangerous," and the lens through which we see the world orients toward scanning the environment for danger. The music teacher may say, "You are out of tune!" and we begin to silence our voice. We experience heartbreak and we begin to guard our heart.

We come to see ourselves a certain way . . . others a certain way . . . life in a certain way. Our views become frozen and static, like a photograph rather than a motion picture. These distorted lenses affect how we see everything and determine our choices, big and small. Often, they operate unconsciously. At other times, we're aware of them, but try as we might, we can't seem to shift them.

Mindfulness practice frees us from past conditioning and habitual patterns. It helps us remove the filters, biases, and preconceived ideas that shape our perceptions and cloud our consciousness. It allows us to see into the nature of reality and comprehend fundamental truths about ourselves and our world. Mindfulness helps us choreograph our life through inner awareness rather than outer reactivity.

When we see clearly, we can respond effectively. To paraphrase Einstein, no problem can be solved by the same kind of thinking that created it.

What does this look like in real life? Jose, whom you met at the start of this chapter, offers an example of how radically mindfulness practice can shift the way we see ourselves and our life.

When Jose began to practice mindfulness, it was as if a light switch was flipped. He became the all-star of mindfulness, dedicating himself to the practices with fierceness and courage. He seemed to "get" mindfulness and how to apply it in his life much faster than I ever did. He was a natural.

As Jose practiced, he began to notice the triggers and early sensations of panic before they erupted into a full-fledged panic attack. He shared about how and when anxiety took hold: "It's thinking about the future, what might happen, that gets me anxious. But nothing has actually happened yet."

Jose also gained perspective on his view of the rival gang members: "They are no different than me. They're just trying to survive, like everyone else."

Most inspiring was the shift in Jose's relationship to himself. This tough young man embraced the mindful attitude of kindness. When his anxiety arose, he didn't shame himself for his "weakness" and "fear" as he had in the past. Instead, he was like a loving father—which he'd never had—comforting a young son.

Jose's mindfulness practice helped him see himself with greater clarity and compassion. Not only did he cure his panic attacks, he healed his life.

The Science of Mindfulness

The healing effects that Jose experienced firsthand have been proven through decades of scientific research across ages, genders, cultures, and life circumstances.

I distinctly remember the first mindfulness study I read about. It involved patients with psoriasis, a very uncomfortable skin disorder.[2] The standard treatment for psoriasis is photo-chemotherapy, which patients receive while standing naked in what looks like an old-fashioned telephone booth. The study looked at what would happen if patients practiced mindfulness while receiving the treatment. Much to my surprise, the results showed that patients who practiced mindfulness cleared their psoriasis 35 percent faster than those not practicing mindfulness. This remarkable result required no added time and almost no added cost, yet it brought huge benefits to the patients.

This study showed me that the power of mindfulness can, indeed, be measured by science. I was eager to learn more. It was my first year in grad school, and I was looking for a research topic for my master's thesis. I knew I wanted to study mindfulness, but I wasn't clear on what aspect I wanted to study or why. Then life unexpectedly provided me direction.

I had had irregular menstrual cycles all my life, and at age twenty-two, I finally gathered the courage to consult my primary care doctor, who quickly referred me to a specialist. The specialist entered the room where I sat waiting, shivering in my exam gown. Without making eye contact, he asked a barrage of questions followed by a physical exam.

Seared into my memory is the doctor saying matter-of-factly, "You may have a tumor in your pituitary." I remember little of the technical jargon that followed, except the devastating conclusion that I might not ever be able to have children.

I was too shocked even for tears.

On a piece of paper, he scrawled information about scheduling an MRI to scan my brain for the possible tumor. I left the building in a daze and have no idea how I drove myself home. It was three long and anxious weeks before I could get the MRI appointment.

The results: no tumor. The wave of relief that coursed through me was replaced by a flood of anger. How could this doctor have been so devoid of empathy and compassion, leaving me for three weeks with no support and no follow-up, to struggle alone with the prospect that I might have a tumor and would never have children?

I began reading about physician burnout. I learned that medical students begin their four-year education with high levels of altruism and compassion, but by their final year, these qualities have dramatically diminished. Medical training was erasing the very qualities at the heart of good doctoring.

This sparked an idea. Since the current training seemed to dehumanize and emotionally disengage doctors, what if mindfulness could protect their humanity by nurturing their empathy and compassion? The direction for my master's thesis was born.

The dean of the medical school approved my research study to offer a "mindfulness elective" to medical students. Eighty students enrolled and were randomly assigned to the mindfulness training or to a wait-list control group. I can still remember the feeling of pure joy when I analyzed the data and saw the results: mindfulness training protected empathy and compassion, and reduced depression and anxiety compared to the control group.

This study, my first, was published in the *Journal of Behavioral Medicine* two decades ago.[3] In the years since, I have continued to research and document the benefits of mindfulness—including improved sleep for people with insomnia, enhanced well-being for women with breast cancer, increased innovation and creativity in engineering students, enhanced ethical decision-making in college students, and reduced stress in high-level professionals. This research is part of the now-significant body of evidence demonstrating the benefits of mindfulness (See Figure 1).

FIGURE 1

The Benefits of Mindfulness

Thousands of studies have shown significant benefits
of mindfulness practice across an array of domains
in psychological, cognitive, and physical health.

Psychological Benefits

Increased happiness[4]

Increased compassion
(for self and other)[5]

Increased life satisfaction[6]

Increased relationship quality[7]

Increased work satisfaction[8]

Increased sense of meaning[9]

Decreased stress[10]

Decreased depression[11]

Decreased anxiety[12]

Cognitive Benefits

Increased attention[13]

Increased memory[14]

Increased creativity[15]

Increased innovation[16]

Reduced mind wandering[17]

Increased problem solving[18]

Increased test scores[19]

Physical Benefits

Improved immune function[20]

Reduced hypertension[21]

Decreased chronic pain[22]

Enhanced epigenetic regulation
of genes to help prevent life-
threatening inflammation[23]

Improved cardiovascular factors,
including cholesterol levels, blood
pressure, and heart function[24]

Decreased levels of cortisol (stress
hormone)[25]

Better sleep quality[26]

Cortical thickening in areas of the
brain associated with attention,
memory, emotional intelligence,
compassion, and empathy[27]

Increased levels of telomerase (an
enzyme that repairs and protects
the ends of DNA strands that keep
us youthful and healthy and slow
aging)[28]

Increased neural integration
in the brain, enabling optimal
functioning[29]

Bottom line: Mindfulness practice is good for you. It increases happiness, empathy, and compassion; improves attention, memory, and the ability to perform on tests; cultivates innovation and creativity; grows areas of the brain related to well-being; and can even slow the aging process by altering our DNA.

Myths About Mindfulness

So how do we harness all of these scientific benefits? The first step is to truly understand what mindfulness is . . . and isn't. Given its soaring popularity and its wide proliferation, there are a great many myths about mindfulness. Below are the top ten myths that I most often hear.

Myth 1: "I'm terrible at mindfulness. My mind wanders all the time."
Truth: Everyone's mind wanders. That's how the mind works. Mindfulness isn't about having a perfectly quiet mind. It's about learning to see the mind clearly, with all of its chaos, confusion, ideas, insights, hopes, and fears.

Myth 2: Mindfulness is just about present-moment attention.
Truth: If mindfulness were only about present-moment attention, then a sniper could be the most mindful person in the world. Mindfulness is about *how* and *why* we pay attention. It involves paying attention with an attitude of kindness and curiosity.

Myth 3: Mindfulness takes too much time.
Truth: Mindfulness actually saves time. It increases your clarity, attention, and effectiveness as you live your day-to-day life. When you are less distracted and make fewer mistakes, you save time.

Myth 4: Mindfulness makes you soft.

Truth: Some clients tell me, "If I get too mindful, I'll lose my edge." In fact, mindfulness will *sharpen* your edge. It enhances your capacity for innovation, learning, and memory. This is a chief reason why Fortune 500 companies and top universities have integrated mindfulness into their organizations.

Myth 5: Mindfulness is passive and won't help me change.

Truth: Mindfulness is not passive or resigned acceptance. Acceptance is simply the first step toward change and growth. We accept situations as they are, not because we want them to be happening, but because they already *are* happening. Through acceptance, we can see our situation clearly instead of getting stuck by denying, worrying, lamenting, or raging about what's happening. When we see things clearly, we respond to them effectively.

Myth 6: Mindfulness is just a stress-management technique.

Truth: Nope, again. Mindfulness is not just a practice for when life is stressful. It enriches all of our moments, big and small, good and bad. As we'll see, it not only helps us through tough times, but also increases and deepens our joyful moments.

Myth 7: Mindfulness is for Buddhists.

Truth: I have learned a great deal from Buddhist teachings, but I'm not a Buddhist. Nor, with rare exceptions, are the people I work with. Although mindfulness has rich roots in Buddhism, it is ultimately a universal, innate human capacity that transcends religion and culture. Anyone can practice and benefit from it.

Myth 8: Mindfulness means you eliminate all your desires and passions.

Truth: Some people misperceive mindfulness as a passionless, go-with-the-flow attitude. As I've noted, mindfulness is not passive resignation, nor is it an elimination of emotion or desire. Mindfulness actually forges a deeper connection with our values and feelings. It wakes us up to life—inside and out—and helps us stay focused on what is most meaningful to us.

Myth 9: Mindfulness is selfish.

Truth: Some clients tell me, "It's selfish to just focus on myself." In fact, the opposite is true. Research shows mindfulness makes us more generous, more compassionate, and better able to support others. Mindfulness helps us recognize our inherent interconnection with each other and all of life. As we deepen this understanding, we realize that we're never just practicing for ourselves, and that our practice has echoes throughout our world.

Myth 10: Mindfulness is just about meditation.

Truth: Meditation strengthens our capacity for mindfulness, much like going to the gym strengthens our muscles. But mindfulness is a way of living, not just a meditation practice. It can be practiced in every moment of our lives, helping us go from *reaction* to *response.*

From Reaction to Response

Have you ever hit "send" on an email and then regretted it a few seconds later? Or snapped at a loved one? Or wished you'd paused before criticizing a colleague?

Reactions like these happen to all of us. Despite our best efforts, we get swept into the raging current of daily life and automatically react to a situation instead of consciously responding. Why does this keep happening, even though we "know better"?

Blame it on our lightning-fast limbic system. This ancient, reptilian part of our brain is typically the first responder to stress, causing us to automatically react instead of skillfully responding from our prefrontal cortex, the seat of higher-order reasoning.

Our self-protective, limbic mechanisms are the product of thousands of years of human experience, transmitted to us through our genes. Our autonomic nervous system regulates a variety of processes that take place without conscious effort, such as breathing or pumping our heart. But when we encounter danger, this same nervous system is responsible for activating our automatic fight, flee, freeze, or faint response.

This emotional reactivity is part of our evolutionary heritage for a reason. It is helpful, indeed essential, when danger is imminent and physical—for example, when a lion is chasing us. But when the danger is psychological in nature, which is more often the case in modern life, this coping mechanism can cause harm.

These reactive patterns are so ingrained that we may not even realize we're engaging in them. Someone cuts us off the on the highway and we _____. Our child forgets to do what we ask for the umpteenth time and we _____. An employee or colleague doesn't do their part of a project and we _____. These patterns can become so dominant that they diminish our capacity to see clearly and limit our freedom to choose a wise and compassionate response. We end up going through life on automatic pilot, cruising along our superhighways of habit, allowing conditioned patterns and emotions to govern what we believe, think, and do.

Mindfulness counters this ingrained reactivity by throwing two powerful blocks into this headlong rush to react:

1. *The mindful pause:* Mindfulness creates a moment of pause between a stimulus and a response. This pause gives us the space to see a situation clearly and *choose* a response, rather than automatically reacting with ingrained patterns that may not serve us, others, or the situation. Mindfulness puts us back in choice. A wise saying attributed to psychologist and Holocaust survivor Viktor Frankl captures it best: "Between the stimulus and response there is a space. In that space is our power to choose our response. In our response lies our growth and our freedom."

2. *The witness state of awareness:* When we pause in mindfulness, we're taking a mental step back from whatever is happening. We can then use our higher-order mind to observe a situation objectively. When we get swept away by the current of life, we lose perspective. Mindfulness helps us rise above the turmoil to see with greater clarity. Imagine being swept away in a raging river. We'd spend all of our energy just trying to keep our head above water. Mindfulness, instead, is like observing the situation from a helicopter. We gain a greater perspective.

> *Mindfulness creates a moment of pause between a stimulus and a response. This pause gives us the space to see a situation clearly and* **choose** *a response.*

Together, the *mindful pause* and the *witness state* free us from our ingrained reactions, especially in emotionally charged situations. While mindfulness does not necessarily change what is happening, it changes our relationship to what is happening. It helps us disembroil ourselves, see the situation with clear eyes, and wisely respond instead of automatically react.

> › *While mindfulness does not necessarily change what is happening, it changes our relationship to what is happening.*

There is a reason why mindfulness practices are being adopted by people from all walks of life. Mindfulness can de-escalate modern stresses of all kinds. It can even be life-saving, as we can see from the following story, shared with me by professor Amishi Jha, one of the pioneers in studying the impact of mindfulness training in the military:[30]

Officer Witt and his squad entered a small village, only to see a group of Afghans coming angrily toward them carrying sticks. The officer said it was mindfulness, the ability to pause instead of automatically react, which gave him the presence of mind to order his men to withhold fire. He commanded them to put their rifles face down on the ground, demonstrating to the villagers that they would not shoot. This act of courage and grace stopped the oncoming villagers. Officer Witt shared that without mindfulness, his fear and reactivity could have taken over. Instead, he prevented a possible massacre.

Full-Spectrum Living

Being human involves the complete spectrum of experience—not just the challenges, but also the boundless beauty. While mindfulness helps us navigate life's tests and trials, it also awakens us to life's joys.

We become more alive to the sights, sounds, sensations, tastes, and emotions of each moment. We find ourselves more able to notice the magical moments in life—the mystery—even in the midst of challenges.

Mindfulness practice keeps us connected with what makes life most meaningful, in touch with what we truly value. More than a tool or a practice, it serves as both a compelling agent of change and a gentle broker of peace.

Mindfulness is a way of perceiving and relating to our world that literally rewires our brain and redesigns the very fabric of our consciousness so we can live with greater happiness, greater compassion, and greater wisdom.

> "To improve the quality of your life, you must improve the quality of your choices. To improve the quality of your choices, you must improve the quality of your thoughts and emotions that produce those choices. To improve the quality of your thoughts and emotions, you must improve the quality of your consciousness. To shift everything, you must shift your consciousness."
>
> BARBARA DE ANGELIS, PHD, *Soul Shifts*

PRACTICE Seeing Clearly

Sit quietly and invite the mind and body to settle. Reflect on the two key mechanisms of mindfulness: the *pause* and the *witness state*. Bring your attention to your breath, and with your next exhale, release any obvious tension you are feeling in your body.

We'll begin by reflecting on a challenging moment from your recent past where you wish you had taken a mindful pause and accessed the witness state. This doesn't have to be a life-changing, make-or-break moment (although you could try this practice with those, too).

Spend several minutes recalling the situation. Bring up the sensory details to help put yourself back in that time and place. Notice the body sensations and emotions that arise as you remember the situation.

Now imagine inserting a gentle pause right in the middle of the difficult situation. Imagine that in this pause you were able to shift your perspective to a more objective witness state.

Notice how this feels. Does it change how you see things? Does it change how you might want to respond? Write down any insights in your journal or on your computer.

Now repeat the practice with a potentially beautiful moment. Imagine the pause, imagine the witness state. Bring all of your senses to bear on this moment. Experience seeing the whole picture. How might you have responded to more fully embrace this moment?

Below are some examples to help you get started:

Challenging moment alternate response: When my boss criticized my work seemingly unfairly, instead of becoming reactive and resentful, I could have paused, felt my upset, and responded by choosing to take a deep breath and speak to her later once I had soothed my emotional reactivity. In this pause, I could attempt to see things more objectively, without shame or blame, and reconnect with what is most important.

Beautiful moment alternate response: When my son was sharing his excitement about his new chemistry experiment, I could have paused to listen and talk with him instead of answering him with my back turned, focused on cooking dinner. In this pause, I could have reconnected to my heart and what was most important: a moment of connection with my son.

GOLD NUGGET Reflect on the highlights from this chapter and then choose one Gold Nugget you want to take with you and encode in your long-term memory. Write this down in your journal.

Sample Gold Nuggets:

- Mindfulness means to see clearly.
- Mindfulness allows us to shift from reaction to response.
- Mindfulness awakens us to life—not just the challenges, but also the boundless beauty.

4

THE THREE PILLARS
OF MINDFULNESS
Intention, Attention, Attitude

Mindfulness is a state of intelligent,
open alertness . . . with a kindly attitude
and a gentle curiosity.

GARY GACH *Pause, Breathe, Smile*

A wonderful Zen teaching hit home for me a few years back: *the most important thing is simply to remember the most important thing.*

I was teaching in Europe and had been away from my then-eight-year-old son, Jackson, for two weeks—the longest we'd ever been apart. On the flight home from Copenhagen, I began feeling guilty for my absence, even suffering pangs of anxiety about our reconnection: *Did I make the wrong choice by leaving for so long? Have I damaged our attachment bond? Does he know I still love him?*

But instead of disappearing down the rabbit hole of motherly guilt, I made a clear intention that when I got home, I wouldn't unpack, check the mail, or catch up on email. I would simply spend my first day reconnecting with Jackson.

I arrived home to a perfect summer Saturday. With the sun pouring through our bay window, Jackson and I decided to spend the day together at the beach. I began gathering our beach gear and preparing a picnic with all his favorite foods. As I was packing up the car, I waved to the neighbors: "Hello! I'm home!" (And, if I'm honest, secretly saying: "See what a good mom I am!")

Finally, I was done. Beach towels, check. Paddleball and soccer ball, check. Sunscreen, check. Perfect picnic, check. Perfect mom, check.

I called to Jackson, who was sitting on our front porch: "Come on, sweetheart, it's time to go to the beach." He didn't respond. I called a bit louder, noticing a hint of impatience in my voice. He didn't even look up.

I felt the tide of impatience rising in my body. *What's this feeling about?* I wondered. In that momentary pause, I realized that somewhere in my mind there was an agenda: *We have to get to the beach before lunchtime, so we can have the perfect sunshine for our perfect picnic for our perfect day—and I can be the perfect mom.*

Then I remembered my intention. Cooped up in a cramped airplane cabin thousands of feet above the earth, all I'd wanted was to get home to my son. To see him, be with him, and let him know: "I'm home. I love you."

I walked over and sat down in the sunshine next to him. He was studying a trail of ants. Their rhythmic march, mundane to most of us in adulthood, fascinated him. As we watched, I sensed myself get quieter inside, more present. I felt the sun on my back, my breath deepening. After a few moments, I felt his little body begin to soften, and as he leaned into me, I realized this was *it*. This moment was the most important thing.

A tear came to my eye as I recognized how close I'd come to missing this moment because of my impatience and reactivity.

The beach, the picnic, the timing—none of it mattered. *This* was what mattered. My little boy, resting against my body, the two of us connected.

It was a brief yet profound lesson in mindfulness for me. Mindfulness reconnects us with our *intention*—with what is most important. It returns our *attention* to the present moment. And it helps us see clearly with an *attitude* of kindness and curiosity, instead of judgment and shame. Mindfulness allows us to see and work with what is happening in the here and now, not some idea of what should be happening.

As I shared in chapter 1, the three pillars of mindfulness are:

- **Intention** puts us in touch with *why* we pay attention.
  It helps us zero in on the most important thing.

- **Attention** helps us train and stabilize
  our focus in the present moment.

- **Attitude** guides *how* we pay attention—
  specifically, with kindness and curiosity.

Intention, attention, and attitude aren't sequential steps or stages. They work together so we can see clearly and respond wisely and compassionately to each moment of life. They help us groove new neural pathways that give us the resources to face life's challenges and deepen life's joys. In this chapter, we'll take a closer look at how and why they work so well.

Intention: *Why* We Pay Attention

Intentions set the compass of our heart in the direction we want to head. They connect us with our personal vision, aspiration, and motivation. Like the rudder on a sailboat, our intentions keep us on course, reminding us again and again of what is most important.

And yet we forget so easily. Swept away by life's business and daily chaos, we lose touch with what is most important. This is why intention is so valuable. It is our personal blueprint, helping us stay connected with what we value most in life, so it is not lost or betrayed.

Remembering our intention puts us back in choice. It reconnects us with our purpose, which then empowers us to make choices that move us toward what we care about most.

In my story with Jackson, setting my intention on the plane primed my brain so that when we were together and the goals I had set for the day were going "wrong" (that is, not according to my best-laid, perfect-mom plans), I could remember my intention and realign myself with what was most important: to connect with my son and let him know how much I love him.

Remembering my intention gave me the crucial pause between my impatience and my response so that I could gain perspective, reconnect with my heart, and choose how I wanted to respond. Mindfulness gave me a precious moment of connection with my son that I never could have planned and that I could have missed entirely if my impatience hadn't been tempered by my intention.

> *Remembering our intention gives us the crucial pause between our reaction and our response so that we can gain perspective, reconnect with our heart, and choose how we want to proceed.*

In fact, intention is so powerful that simply setting an intention can make us happier. Research has demonstrated that setting the intention to be happy elevated dopamine levels in the brain, creating or extending positive mood.[1] Dopamine is one of the key neurotransmitters (brain chemicals) responsible for feelings of happiness and is widely regarded as the brain's reward system.

Recent research also has found a significant link between positive intentions and better memory. Interestingly, the word mindfulness is often translated as "to remember," and research shows that mindfulness practice is associated with increased working memory—what's written on the whiteboard of your mind. As we increase our working memory, we are making our deepest values and intentions more readily available in daily life.

> *Mindfulness practice is associated with increased working memory—what's written on the whiteboard of your mind.*

For example, if in the morning I set an intention to be present with my son, mindfulness helps me stay connected with this intention by strengthening my access to my working memory. That way whenever I look, I see in beautiful writing "Jackson is precious" across the whiteboard of my mind. Mindfulness helps us stay connected to our desires and aspirations by helping us remember our deepest intentions.

Isn't it incredible that just the act of setting an intention will improve how we feel, how well we think and solve problems, and how well we remember?

> *Just the act of setting an intention will improve how we feel, how well we think and solve problems, and how well we remember.*

Before we move on to discuss attention, I'd like to pause for a moment and ask you to look back at your intention from chapter 1. See if this intention still feels right, or if it has changed and evolved. Reflect on the question, "In what direction do I want to set the compass of my heart?" Listen for whatever intention is most true for you now. Write it down.

Attention: Training and Stabilizing Our Focus in the Present

In Las Vegas casinos, there are often signs posted: "You must be present to win." The same is true in life: you have to be present in order to truly experience its richness, beauty, and meaning. In fact, this moment, right now, is the only one we have for sure.

Yet so often we're propelled into the future or sucked into the past, and we miss the present moment. In the story I shared, I almost missed the moment with Jackson because I was so focused on my future agenda at the beach. Mindfulness helps us return our attention to the present moment.

For example, try focusing your attention on the sensations in your right hand. Notice how you suddenly have awareness of your right hand. A moment ago, your right hand was not in your awareness. Now, shift your attention to your left hand. Notice how you now have awareness of your left hand. **Where we focus our attention becomes our life.**

Which is not to say that being present is easy. We live with so much stimulus and distraction, it's a wonder we can think clearly at all. A 2012 study revealed that our brains are bombarded by the equivalent of more than *forty gigabytes* of incoming information every day.[2] An average HD movie consists of three to four gigabytes. Imagine trying to absorb and comprehend in detail ten to thirteen movies each day. There is literally not enough time to take in and process that much information.

Not surprisingly, this fire-hose level of input hinders our capacity to pay attention. As cognitive scientist Herbert Simon eloquently notes, "What information consumes is attention. A wealth of information means a poverty of attention."[3]

In our efforts to spread our attention over more information than we can possibly absorb, many of us have developed a workaround that has become an accepted part of modern life: multitasking. Unfortunately, research has revealed—and most of us know full well from experience—that, despite our belief that we can be more productive and effective doing two (or more!) things at once, our brains simply cannot multitask.

When we talk on the phone while checking email or switch back and forth between texting and reading a book, what the brain actually does when attempting to multitask is "spotlight"—constantly jump back and forth between the tasks. Each time the brain switches its spotlight, there's a time cost. As the American Psychological Association notes, "although switching costs may be relatively small, sometimes as little as a few tenths of a second per switch, they can add up to a large amount . . . and can cost as much as 40% of someone's productive time."[4]

Further, research demonstrates that multitaskers made twice as many mistakes and took three times as long to complete their tasks.[5] To make matters worse, the constant toggling between tasks released a rush of cortisol, resulting in increased stress and reported fatigue.[6]

Despite our best efforts to fool ourselves into thinking otherwise, multitasking is in fact one of the greatest enemies to being effective and is bad for your health. Worst of all, it causes us to miss out on the precious moments of life that are right in front of us. As the quote often attributed to Einstein goes, "If you can drive safely while kissing a girl, you are simply not giving the kiss the attention it deserves."

Try this simple exercise: First, say the alphabet. Second, count to 26. Next, try to multitask: say one letter and count one number in sequence—A, 1, B, 2, C, 3, et cetera. How much faster did you go and how much better did you feel when you focused on one thing at a time?

Productive, effective action starts with seeing situations clearly. To see clearly, we must stabilize our minds in the present. Psychologist and Harvard professor Chris Germer noted, "An unstable mind is like an unstable camera; we get a fuzzy picture."[7]

But even when we let go of multitasking, seeing clearly still isn't always easy—because it turns out that the deluge of information isn't just coming from the outside.

Research from Harvard finds that on average, our minds wander 47 percent of the time. Think about that for a moment. That is *almost half* of our lives we are missing. So, in addition to the forty gigabytes of information bombarding us from the world around us, our brains generate between fifty thousand to seventy thousand thoughts per day. That's more than one thought every two seconds, assuming you're awake for all twenty-four hours of the day.

> *Our minds wander 47 percent of the time. That is almost half our lives!*

This phenomenon, as I've mentioned, is called "monkey mind" because our mind behaves like a monkey, constantly swinging from thought to thought. We get swept into fears of a future that doesn't yet exist or lost in ruminations of a past that's already gone. Consequently, we miss the present moment: the only moment that actually exists. Everything else is just mental fabrication.

What's more, when our monkey mind makes mischief by obsessing about the future or ruminating about the past, it floods our bodies with cortisol, aka "the stress hormone." High cortisol levels cause hypertension, weaken our immune system, cause fat deposits, and reduce libido (among other detriments).

Mindfulness helps tame our monkey mind. As we train and stabilize our attention, we begin to see more clearly. Our brain becomes more stable and we become more effective at managing the daily data influx, as well as better at enjoying the moment at hand.

Not only do we become more effective, we become happier.

A famous study by psychologists Matthew Killingsworth and Daniel Gilbert demonstrated that when our minds wander, we're more likely to be unhappy. They studied fifteen thousand people across eighty countries of varying levels of education, age, occupation, incomes, and marital status. Throughout the day, at random times, participants were contacted via their cell phones and asked what activity they were involved in, whether or not their mind was wandering while performing the activity, and to rate their current happiness level.

The study found that what makes us happy has far less to do with what we're doing and far more to do with whether or not we're present. For example, if you are present while washing dishes, even if you don't much like doing dishes, you'll be happier than if your mind is lost in the future or in the past, even if you're thinking about a vacation in Hawaii. As the researchers concluded, "a wandering mind is an unhappy mind."[8]

The converse is also true: *a present mind is a happy mind.* We can bring greater happiness into our lives by simply being present. (More about this in chapter 9).

Bottom line: Whatever you're doing, whether you love it or loathe it, you'll be happiest and most effective if you are present.

Attitude: *How* We Pay Attention

Of the three pillars of mindfulness, attitude is the one most often overlooked. While intention reminds us what is most important and attention stabilizes our mind in the present, our attitude affects how we pay attention. *How* we pay attention determines our ability to see clearly, to learn effectively, and to respond wisely and compassionately.

Mindfulness involves bringing a kind and curious attitude to whatever we are experiencing, like a loving parent or grandparent, welcoming all of our experience.

As a young girl, I remember every time I walked through my grandparents' door, Grandpa would enthusiastically shout, "Shauna!!!" And Nana would chime in, "Tell us everything!" Such unconditional love—all of me welcome, the heartbreaks, the triumphs, and every moment in between. Their *listening love* was the attitude of mindfulness in action.[9]

In fact, kindness is woven into the very fabric of the word "mindfulness" and is what gives this practice its power and capacity for transformation. The Japanese character for mindfulness comprises two interactive figures: one is "presence," the other is "heart" or "mind." Therefore, an equally accurate translation of mindfulness is *heartfulness.* This underscores the importance of cultivating an openhearted attitude as part of our practice.

One of my great concerns about the mindfulness "revolution" is that it often neglects this crucial pillar of attitude. People often think of "the kindness part" as a side note or something nice to have; or worse, they mistakenly believe it will make them soft and cause them to lose their edge.

In fact, the opposite is true.

It turns out that an attitude of kindness and curiosity is directly linked to performance and well-being. Basically, it works this way: the brain is made up of a trillion cells floating in a chemical solution called cerebrospinal fluid. Thoughts, emotions, and sensations are molecules interacting with each other in this chemical solution. Our attitude changes the chemical environment in which these molecules interact and connect.

> *An attitude of kindness and*
> *curiosity is directly linked to*
> *performance and well-being.*

When the stress response is activated in the brain, it releases a cascade of sympathetic neurotransmitters such as adrenaline and cortisol. These chemicals or "threat hormones" create a stressed chemical environment in which molecules of thought, emotion, and sensation are negatively shaped.

In contrast, an attitude of kindness activates the relaxation response in the brain, which releases parasympathetic neurotransmitters such as acetylcholine, endorphins, and oxytocin. Even if you are in a difficult situation, simply adding the resonance of kindness changes the chemical soup.

These chemicals create a healthy environment in which molecules of thought, emotion, and sensation are shaped. An attitude of kindness and curiosity enables the learning and information-processing areas of the brain to function more effectively. The result? We can more objectively evaluate our situation so that we can effectively respond.

This becomes especially crucial in difficult times. Tough times elicit all sorts of challenging emotions—sadness, anger, and fear, to name just a few. Many of us have been trained to not pay attention to these feelings—to ignore them or even deny their existence. Mostly this happens because we "don't want to feel sad," or we don't want to acknowledge that we are angry or afraid.

But remember: *what we practice grows stronger*. Practicing denial and avoidance only strengthens our habits of denial and avoidance. It does nothing to help us resolve difficult situations. It also causes the areas of our brain responsible for regulating difficult emotions to atrophy over time. Then, when we inevitably encounter a challenge we can't ignore, we lack the tools to respond wisely and effectively.

Practicing kindness and curiosity gives us a healthy, compassionate, and effective alternative to shutting down, imploding, or exploding when we encounter challenging events or emotions. When we learn to meet our pain (or fear, anger, loneliness, boredom, guilt, jealousy, shame, embarrassment, or disgust) with kindness and curiosity, we learn to treat ourselves like our own best friend. **We become our inner ally instead of our inner enemy.**

> ⟩ *Practicing kindness and curiosity gives us a healthy, compassionate, and effective alternative to shutting down, imploding, or exploding when we encounter challenging events or emotions.*

Think about how you would treat a young child in pain. Would you say, "Stop that! What's wrong with you?" Or would you embrace this suffering child and say, "Sweetheart, this is hard. Tell me about it. I care."

This attitude of kindness and curiosity toward our inner experience does not sugarcoat our emotions or try to suppress or change them. Instead, it allows us to experience our emotions in a safe, loving way. Paradoxically, by welcoming our experience without initially trying to change it, we actually change everything.

It might seem surprising that kindness and curiosity can bring about great change, but modern neuroscience is proving it. Studies show that when we are judgmental and shaming instead of kind and curious, the learning centers of the brain shut down, shuttling resources to our survival centers and robbing us of the resources we need to effectively respond.

> *When we are judgmental and shaming instead of kind and curious, the learning centers of the brain shut down, shuttling resources to our survival centers and robbing us of the resources we need to effectively respond.*

In contrast, David Rigoni and his colleagues found that an attitude of kindness strengthens the learning centers of the brain, bathing our system in dopamine—one of the brain's neurotransmitters responsible for learning and rewards.[10] This expands our perspective and opens us to greater creativity and resourcefulness. Further research has found that when people are curious about a subject, they're better at learning the information and remembering it, in part because curiosity activates our reward system.[11]

Not only are we better learners when we activate our inner kindness and curiosity, but we're better innovators, too. A recent study of engineers and engineering students that my colleagues and I conducted at Stanford University found that a mindful (i.e., open, kind, curious) attitude was the strongest predictor of innovation.[12]

Finally, researchers have identified curiosity as a significant factor for stress tolerance and as protection against depression. New research shows that depression is linked to a lack of novelty and curiosity. Evidence suggests that people who are suffering from depression have a shrunken hippocampus and are unable to recognize novelty. Interestingly, dopamine levels spike when the brain encounters novelty, which activates pleasure centers and encourages us to learn and explore. Research shows that an attitude of curiosity enables increased growth-related behaviors and a sense of greater meaning and life satisfaction.[13]

This research is revolutionary. Science is showing that the path to a happier and more fulfilled life starts with grooving an attitude of kindness and curiosity into our brains. This is something we can practice and grow.

> *Science is showing that the path to a happier and more fulfilled life starts with grooving an attitude of kindness and curiosity into our brains.*

Formal Practice: Mindfulness Meditation

There are two ways you can put everything we've been discussing into practice: *formal* and *informal practice*.

Informal practice can infuse our everyday life, as we bring Intention, Attention, and Attitude into each moment—for example, mindful eating, mindful reading (which you're doing right now!), mindful driving. We'll discuss informal practice in detail in chapter 9.

Formal practice takes multiple forms. The most widely studied and practiced is sitting meditation, which we will learn below.

People often wonder when is the best time to practice. While you can practice at any time that works for you, when we first awaken in the morning, we have a unique opportunity. During these first few minutes, your mind and brain are very still and receptive. It is a wonderful time to influence and shape your brain for the good. Instead of planning or worrying about our day, we can begin by building our inner resources.

It can also be helpful to practice just before going to bed. This is a skillful way to let go of the stress of the day and shift into sleep. Interestingly, research by professor Elissa Epel at University of California, San Francisco, found that positive mood in the morning and especially at night is correlated with better mitochondria functioning. Mitochondria are considered the body's battery, its energy source. There are around one thousand mitochondria in every cell and we need to keep them healthy. Thus, engaging in practices upon arising and going to sleep seem to be an important ingredient for healthy living.

And yet, often it's hard to make time to practice. There are a million other things we "need" to do. It can be challenging to make sitting still a priority. I know this firsthand—especially on those days when I'm super busy and have a hundred things to get done and my mind is racing *(I really should be finishing the next chapter of my book, or doing the laundry, or helping Jackson study, or . . .).*

It helps to remind myself of all the benefits I'm getting just from sitting still and taking the time to practice: *By doing this, I'm strengthening my immune system, decreasing my levels of cortisol, enhancing my empathy and compassion, increasing my memory and capacity to learn, fostering emotional intelligence, improving my sleep quality, enhancing my relationships, boosting my vitality, and making myself a better citizen of the world. Whew, that sounds like a pretty good way to spend my time!*

I don't mean to imply that we need science to tell us that meditation practice is good for us. You will experience its benefits for yourself. But on those days when a little reminder is needed to carve out the time, I hope my own mental pep talk helps you to stop, sit, breathe, and give yourself the gift of these mindful minutes.

One last thing. Mindfulness practice is not about creating or changing anything about your experience. It is changing the way you *relate to* your experience by adding the resonance of intention, attention, and attitude.

How to Begin a Meditation Practice

Just like with any other habit we want to form, we must follow a few basic guidelines:

- Create a clear intention.

- Commit to an attainable goal, e.g. five minutes per day that you schedule in your calendar.

- Find a place to practice that is quiet and supportive.

- Practice every day. Daily practice is crucial for developing a habit.

- Remember to be kind and curious.

PRACTICE **Mindfulness Meditation Practice Instructions**

You may read through these instructions and then gently guide yourself, or you can choose to listen online (drshaunashapiro.com).

If you are guiding yourself, set a quiet timer for the number of minutes you have committed to practicing. Sit quietly, making sure that your spine is straight and upright (but not tense) and that your body feels supported. Allow your eyes to close, or let your gaze rest in a relaxed way on a spot on the floor in front of you.

Intention: Begin by setting your intention for practice. It is helpful to say your intention to yourself, aloud or silently. For example: "May this practice bring greater peace and clarity into my life" or "May this help me be more present and kind" or simply: "May this be of benefit."

Attention: Focus your attention in the present moment. Gently scan your body and release any obvious tension, especially in the jaw and shoulders. See if you can soften 5 percent more. Allow a gentle smile to rest on your lips.

Notice that you are breathing. Don't try to change the breath; simply experience it. Feel the breath as it naturally flows in and out of your body.

See how carefully and continuously you can feel the sensations of the inhalation and exhalation, from the very beginning all the way to its most subtle end. Allow the breath to breathe itself. No need to control it.

When you notice your mind wandering, use your breath as an anchor, and gently guide your mind back to it again and again. By doing this, you are training your mind to focus, to place itself in the present moment.

Attitude: Infuse your attention with the attitudes of kindness and curiosity. See if you can bring 5 percent more kindness, interest, and caring to this experience. It's especially helpful to notice the tone of your inner voice when your mind wanders off. See if you can bring your attention back with an attitude of kindness and curiosity. Treat your wayward mind like a little puppy, patiently and persistently telling it, "Come back . . . stay . . . stay . . . that's right . . ."

Just the intention to bring kindness to the moment is healing and softens our heart. Every time we gently begin again, we are laying down the neural pathways for mindfulness. Rather than striving for perfection, we are practicing 5 percent more kindness, 5 percent more attention, 5 percent more clarity.

When it is time for the meditation practice to end, notice how you feel. Take a moment to let the sensation of this unique awareness soak in. Just like a wholesome meal, take the time to digest the nourishment. Know that you are absorbing the nutrients of the present moment and trust that out of this richness will come new answers.

Gently allow your eyes to open and bring movement into your body. As you rise and continue with your day, see if you can bring a seamless continuity of mindful presence with you into each moment. Notice that *even as the meditation ends, the mindfulness continues*. Practice bringing intention, attention, and attitude into each moment of your life.

Common Questions about Formal Mindfulness Meditation Practice

1. **My mind wandered. I'm terrible at this.**
   What can I do? It's natural for the mind to wander. Remember, the mind wanders an average 47 percent of the time. The key is how you bring it back. Can you bring it back with kindness, with curiosity, with compassion? Treating your mind tenderly, as you would a little puppy who continually wanders off: "Come back . . . stay . . ."

2. **Why do I feel so tired when I meditate?** I hear this from thousands of people. You want to know why you feel so tired when you meditate? It's because you *are* tired. Remember, mindfulness is about seeing clearly. Most of us are sleep deprived. Mindfulness helps bring our attention to our sleepiness, so we can respond effectively and compassionately to it.

3. **How do I handle physical or emotional pain?** First, simply acknowledge the pain with kindness, welcoming the pain as you would a young child in need of care. Then you can begin to explore the pain with gentle curiosity: *What does this sadness/hurt/ loneliness feel like? Perhaps there's a tightening in my throat or chest; perhaps a tear in my eye. Can I create a container of loving awareness to hold the experience?* We are like a parent who says to her child who scraped her knee, "Oh, sweetheart, I know it hurts. Tell me about it. I care."

4. *How much do I have to practice?* This is another question
    I'm often asked. You already know that what you practice
    grows stronger. Research on meditation practice supports
    this: more practice = more improvement. However, if
    you want a specific number, current research shows a
    threshold effect at twelve minutes. In other words, we see
    improvement in physical health and mental happiness
    in those who meditate for at least twelve minutes per
    day. However, people who meditate longer receive
    proportionately greater benefits. I recommend starting
    with one minute a day for a week and working your way
    up. The key is to make a commitment that you know you
    will be able to meet. You need to be able to trust yourself
    and your word.

GOLD NUGGET   Pause and reflect on the highlights from
this chapter and then choose one Gold Nugget you want to
take with you and encode in your long-term memory. Write it
down in your journal.

Sample Gold Nuggets:

- The most important thing is to remember
  the most important thing.
- You must be present to win.
- Kindness and curiosity turn on the
  learning centers of the brain.

PART 2

When the Going Gets Tough, the Tough Get Compassionate

SELF-COMPASSION

Your Inner Ally

We need to see how the habit of constant
self-judgment diminishes our life force,
steals our inner peace, and crushes our souls.
FRANK OSTASESKI

Unlike self-criticism,
which asks if you're good enough,
self-compassion asks what's good for you?
KRISTIN NEFF, PHD

Straight out of grad school and ready to save the world, I walked into the Veteran's Hospital in Tucson, Arizona, for my first day leading a therapy group for soldiers with PTSD. Even though I was aware of the shocking statistic that each year we lose more soldiers to suicide than to combat, I was entirely unprepared for the depth of suffering and despair I encountered. I was also unprepared for the ocean of compassion these soldiers had for each other.

But there was one man in the group who never said a word. Week after week, he just stared at the floor.

Then one day he raised his hand. All eyes turned toward him as he cleared his throat and slowly uttered words I had never heard: "I don't want to get better."

He continued: "What I saw in the war, what I did . . . I don't deserve to get better."

He looked back down at the floor. Then, in excruciating detail, he described what he had seen and what he had done.

As he spoke, the chill of his shame filled the room. Slowly, he raised his eyes to meet the gaze of his fellow soldiers. Instead of the rejection and judgment he expected, he found compassion.

He didn't say another word, but as he rose to leave, I got the feeling that something inside him had begun to thaw. Slowly, over the next weeks, the compassion of the other men helped him find compassion for himself. He began to believe that he wasn't defined by his past actions. He began to believe that change was possible, that there was a path out of his suffering.

I continued to work with this soldier for months. After his last session, he shared this:

> The military trains you to survive in combat. When you're there, you rely on your training, and you trust your instincts. But nothing can prepare you to fight against yourself. How do you fight a battle when the good guy and the bad guy are the same guy?
>
> I've finally realized that fighting won't lead to peace. I will never forget what happened, but I'm not going to waste any more energy beating myself up for it. I still have life inside of me and I want to live it for something bigger than myself.

This veteran's words reveal the power of self-compassion: regardless of our past, compassion can help us rediscover our dignity and our purpose. The revolutionary act of treating ourselves kindly can begin to reverse years or even a lifetime of self-judgment and shame. Like a guiding light, self-compassion allows us to face our darkness.

> > *Like a guiding light, self-compassion*
> > *allows us to face our darkness.*

Self-Compassion: What It Is, What It Does, Why It's Radical

Dr. Kristin Neff, a professor from the University of Texas at Austin who first defined and measured the construct of self-compassion, says that self-compassion involves treating ourselves as we would treat a dear friend who is having a hard time. We learn to bring kindness, affection, and tenderness to our own suffering. We discover that we can be on our own team, instead of berating or rejecting ourselves.

We can even learn to be kind to ourselves when we're in the wrong—not because we're letting ourselves off the hook, but because we're hurting. Self-compassion offers a radical approach: *You don't have to be perfect to be worthy of love and kindness.*

If you're wondering how to start being kinder toward yourself, there is good news—you've already learned the first step: mindfulness. Self-compassion is born of mindfulness. We can't be kind to ourselves unless we first acknowledge we are in pain. In tough times, mindfulness helps us see our suffering clearly. Self-compassion adds: "Be kind to yourself in the midst of suffering."[1]

Self-compassion does more than just help us feel better. It provides us the life raft we need to navigate through the tough times.

By deepening our self-compassion, we discover untapped reserves of strength, resilience, and wisdom that help us survive the storm, *and* we strengthen our resources to better navigate future storms. This is one of the alchemical powers of self-compassion: it simultaneously soothes the negative and grows the positive.

Yet, sadly, self-compassion is not our typical response when the going gets tough. Instead, we tend to fall back on habitual coping mechanisms that are ineffective and can be downright harmful.

Our Two Most Common (and ineffective) Coping Mechanisms

When faced with adversity, many of us respond in one of two ways. We either turn on ourselves, our minds filled with self-judgment and shame. Or we try to paper over mistakes with rationalizations and pep talks intended to boost our self-esteem.

These coping strategies don't work because both are defense mechanisms that distract us from the underlying issues. When we're knocked down or we've made a mistake, we think the key is to take a tough-love, hoist-ourselves-up-by-the-bootstraps attitude. But if we can't see our behavior patterns clearly, we just keep repeating them.

Here's where self-compassion comes to the rescue. It gives us the courage to face painful underlying issues and to make the changes needed to heal them.

Shame. Doesn't. Work.

Many of us carry deep feelings of personal deficiency. We criticize ourselves relentlessly. As cartoonist Jules Feiffer put it: "I grew up to have my father's looks, my father's speech patterns, my father's posture, my father's walk, my father's opinions, and my mother's contempt for my father."[2]

When things go awry, most of us shame ourselves about our shortcomings and imperfections, mistakenly believing this will somehow motivate us to change. This habitual response is problematic for two main reasons.

First, when we are hurting is precisely when we most need compassion, not a kick in the pants. Shame not only feels crummy, but it also literally robs our brain of the resources it needs to respond effectively to the challenging situation.

When we feel shame, the amygdala—the part of our brain that is central to memory, decision-making, and emotional responses—triggers a cascade of norepinephrine and cortisol, chemicals that increase our stress level, narrow our perspective on perceived "threats," and inhibit our cognitive flexibility. Shame puts us in the grip of our fight, flight, or freeze survival response, thereby inhibiting the learning centers of the brain.

If we want to learn from our mistakes and keep from repeating them, we need a compassionate mind-set, not shame. For example, I remember arriving late one day to pick Jackson up from school. He was the last child waiting. When I saw him sitting there, cold, lonely, and miserable, shame started its toxic tirade: *Why didn't you schedule your day more carefully! Now look at what you've done. You are failing as a mother.*

> *If we want to learn from our mistakes and keep from repeating them, we need a compassionate mind-set, not shame.*

While it's natural to feel regret about making a mistake, especially if it causes pain to someone else, if I fall prey to these judgmental thoughts, not only are they adding to the pain I already feel for being late, but they're also preventing me from being attuned to Jackson as he gets in the car and inhibiting my ability to learn from the situation and handle it differently in the future.

What I really needed was: *Oh, sweetheart, it is painful to see Jackson sitting alone waiting for you. Next time, remember not to squeeze one more student meeting into office hours.* Followed by a deep breath to help me reset and be the present, loving mother I want to be as I pick up my son.

When you bring a compassionate response to a difficult situation instead of shaming yourself, you're more likely to learn from your mistakes and proactively work on making changes.

A second reason shame is problematic is that it often leads to self-sabotage in just the ways we're hoping to avoid. When we denigrate the parts of ourselves that most need kind attention, those disowned parts of us don't just go away. They linger in our subconscious, only to sabotage us later, when we least expect it. This is why many of us, despite recognizing and verbalizing our flaws or failings, continue to make the same mistakes again and again, despite our best intentions.

Consider yo-yo dieters, for example. They strive to reduce their calorie intake and even succeed for a while, but once they break their diet (an inevitability at some point), they often turn on themselves, lose all self-confidence, and give up. They think, *I might as well eat the whole pint of ice cream, since I've messed up my diet anyway.*

Of course, that makes them feel worse: *I'm so weak, I'm such a pig.* Then they eat even more, because food becomes a source of comfort and temporary relief from the toxic tirade within. It's a vicious cycle.

The change-inducing effects of self-compassion were demonstrated in a study by Mark Leary and colleagues at Duke

University.[3] After female dieters were asked to eat a doughnut, half of the participants were told, "Several people have told me that they feel bad about eating doughnuts in this study, so I hope you won't be hard on yourself." The other participants, those in the control group, weren't told anything.

The researchers found that those who were in the control group were very hard on themselves after eating the doughnut (they reported feeling guilty and ashamed), whereas participants who were encouraged to be self-compassionate about eating the doughnut were kinder to themselves and less upset after eating it. What's more, when they were later given the opportunity to eat as much candy as they wanted as part of a "taste testing" session, they ate less candy than those in the control group.

Self-compassion supported these women in remaining focused on their goal of eating healthfully after a temporary stumble, instead of giving way to self-indulgence.

Yale professor Sidney Blatt has found that much of depression is due to self-criticism—beating ourselves up when we feel we aren't performing well enough.[4] Instead of helping us grow and evolve, shame undermines our belief in ourselves, marooning us on an island of helplessness and self-loathing. As Brené Brown aptly puts it, "Shame corrodes the very part of us that believes we are capable of change."[5]

In contrast, when we act with self-compassion, we trigger the release of oxytocin—the love hormone that facilitates safety and connection, and endorphins—our natural, feel-good neurotransmitters. Together, these reduce distress and increase feelings of care and support. Psychologist Paul Gilbert from the University of Derby proposes that when we practice self-compassion, we are deactivating the threat-defense system and activating the care system.[6]

> *When we act with self-compassion,*
> *we trigger the release of oxytocin—*
> *the love hormone that facilitates safety*
> *and connection, and endorphins—*
> *our natural, feel-good neurotransmitters.*

Despite its benefits, self-compassion is often difficult for many of us. We're far more compassionate toward others than toward ourselves. If a friend comes to us with a problem, do we yell at our friend for being stupid and incompetent? Of course not. We offer compassion when our friend has made a mistake. Yet we react with self-judgment and shame when we're having a hard time.

Shame doesn't help us. It only harms us. Shaming ourselves is like picking up a hot coal: it will burn you. So, the next time you reach for a critical, judgmental thought, protect yourself, just as you would protect a dear friend or a young child reaching for a hot coal: "No, that will burn you."

Self-Esteem Doesn't Work, Either

For decades, self-help literature has been flooded with exhortations and exercises to bolster self-esteem as the answer to surviving life's stresses. Millions of dollars have been poured into schools to boost our children's self-esteem, with the goal of strengthening their resilience in the face of challenge. Unfortunately, as well-meant as these efforts are, science is revealing that self-esteem is neither an effective nor a healthy approach to dealing with tough times, especially when compared to the power of self-compassion.

While both self-esteem and self-compassion have been strongly linked to psychological well-being, there's a crucial difference between them: *self-esteem needs success to prove your self-worth, whereas self-compassion says you are worthy no matter what*. Self-esteem is inherently unstable, rising and falling according to our latest success or failure. It is a fair-weather friend: supporting us when we're doing well, but abandoning us when something goes awry and we need support the most. Self-esteem also triggers constant comparison to determine self-worth—*am I better than you or worse than you?*—which erodes cooperation and leads to the idea that in order for someone to "win," someone else has to "lose."

> *Self-esteem needs success to prove your self-worth, whereas self-compassion says you are worthy no matter what.*

Self-compassion, in contrast, is constant. Like a staunch friend, it unflaggingly relates with kindness and acceptance to the ever-changing landscape of who we are, even when we fail or feel inadequate. With self-compassion in our corner, we have a constant ally, there for us precisely when self-esteem deserts us.

Research bears out these points. It shows that people with high self-compassion have a stable sense of self-worth, whereas in people with high self-esteem, self-worth is volatile and fluctuates depending on what is happening in their lives. When they experience external successes, they experience higher self-worth, but when they experience failure, their self-worth plummets.

At the University of California, Berkeley, researchers administered an impossibly hard spelling test that all the students failed. Half the students were encouraged to be self-compassionate ("Try not to be too hard on yourself" or "It's common for students to have difficulty with tests like these"). The other half were given statements designed to boost their self-esteem ("You must be intelligent if you got into Berkeley!").

The students who were encouraged to be self-compassionate ended up being more successful on the next test. Why? Because, thanks to self-compassion, they didn't see the first failed test as a failure, but as an opportunity to learn. As a result, they likely spent more time studying because they weren't devastated by the previous failure.

In contrast, the students who were given the self-esteem-boosting statements were more affected by their previous failure and felt it futile to study. The lead researcher, Juliana Breines, summarized the findings: "We found that people who were taught to be kind to themselves felt more motivated to see their mistakes as a chance for growth."[7]

People with high self-esteem may not be as resilient because when something goes wrong, their self-confidence is shattered. Few people realize that self-compassion is a key ingredient in resilience. Angela Duckworth, whose book, *Grit*, I mentioned previously, prizes self-compassion and a nonjudgmental attitude as essential characteristics of grit. It's not that people who are self-compassionate expect less of themselves — research shows that their standards are as high as anyone else's. The key difference is that self-compassionate individuals know that it's okay to fail — indeed, their very definition of failure is different. Failing is simply an opportunity to learn. I discovered a wonderful Japanese saying in Duckworth's book: "Fall seven, rise eight." No matter how many times we fall, we can rise again.

Self-compassion promotes this kind of resilience and the courage to continue after mistakes, setbacks, and failures. It may seem counterintuitive, but the gentle touch of self-compassion rather than self-esteem builds the sturdy backbone we call grit.

So, the next time you've made a mistake or are facing something difficult, instead of expending valuable resources in self-blame (*What was I thinking? What's wrong with me?*) or denying anything's wrong (*Get over it! Suck it up! It's all good*), see if you can pause, recognize you're in pain, and offer yourself compassion. You may see what has happened through a different lens, as a doorway for learning and growth: *What can I learn? How can I grow?*

This compassionate perspective helps point the compass in a constructive direction, more toward "Where do I go from here?" rather than self-blame.

Relearning and Reteaching Loveliness

The willingness to face the darker parts of ourselves and the darker parts of life takes courage. This courage is born of compassion — compassion for ourselves and for each other. As we practice self-compassion, we learn not only to confront and grow from our own struggles and sorrows, but to connect with the sufferings and sorrows of others. When we offer compassion to others, we allow them the possibility of finding compassion and growth for themselves.

In fact, sometimes the most powerful moments of self-compassion are catalyzed through receiving compassion from others. Think back to the veteran we talked about at the beginning of this chapter. The compassion he received from the other men in the group, after sharing his most shameful moment, served as a turning point in his recovery from PTSD.

Self-compassion teaches us to embrace the human quality of imperfection. As Kristin Neff succinctly put it, "You don't have to be special to have self-compassion. You just have to be a mess like every other human being."[8]

In essence, compassion is about love. It is treating ourselves with love, letting ourselves feel loved despite doubt, imperfection, and darkness. It is about relearning our own loveliness. Poet Galway Kinnell beautifully captures this:

> everything flowers, from within, of self-blessing;
> though sometimes it is necessary
> to reteach a thing its loveliness,
> to put a hand on its brow . . .
> and retell it in words and in touch
> it is lovely
> until it flowers again from within, of self-blessing

PRACTICE   **Compassionate Letter to Myself**

To begin practicing self-compassion, it can be helpful to write a letter to yourself about a current struggle in your life, or an area where you feel inadequate and want to motivate yourself to change. But this letter has a special twist. In this letter to yourself, write *as if you were talking to a dear friend* facing the same concerns as you. How might you respond to your friend? What might you say? How might you support her?[9]

Tip: Try not to think too much about organizing your words or thoughts. Simply write from your heart.

After writing the letter, put it in an envelope and mail it to yourself. When you receive it, see if you can slowly re-read it, letting the words soothe and comfort you.

GOLD NUGGET   Pause and reflect on the highlights from this chapter and then choose one Gold Nugget you want to take with you and encode in your long-term memory. Write it down in your journal.

Sample Gold Nuggets:

- Shame shuts down the learning centers of your brain.
- Self-esteem is a fair-weather friend.
- Self-compassion is a powerful ally.

THE FIVE ROADBLOCKS TO SELF-COMPASSION
How to Overcome Them

Self-love is the only "diet" that truly works.
JENNY CRAIG

Never compare your insides
to everyone else's outsides.
ANNE LAMOTT

The research is clear: self-compassion is a much more effective and healthy approach than shame or self-esteem. People with greater self-compassion have less depression, anxiety, and stress—and greater happiness, life satisfaction, optimism, resilience, and performance.[1]

Yet when I suggest self-compassion as a practice, people often balk. They're afraid that self-compassion will let them off the hook for their mistakes and they'll lose their drive and motivation to change.

These fears are understandable. But they're based in fiction, not fact.

Below I'll show why the most common misgivings about self-compassion are fundamentally wrong. From there, we'll dive more deeply into how to practice self-compassion and build this valuable resource each of us has within.

Misgivings about Self-Compassion

It Undermines Motivation

One of the biggest blocks to self-compassion is the belief that if we don't criticize ourselves for failing to live up to our standards, we'll lose our motivation to change.

Science shows just the opposite. Self-compassion provides the optimal mental and physical environment to motivate us, providing the sense of safety and encouragement needed to face tough issues.

In a study by Helen Rockliff and colleagues, participants were asked to imagine a difficult situation.[2] Half were left alone to dwell on the details of the situation, while the other half were repeatedly reminded by the researchers, "Allow yourself to feel that you are the recipient of great compassion; allow yourself to feel the lovingkindness that is there for you."

The participants who were reminded to be compassionate had lower cortisol levels, indicating lower levels of stress from imagining the difficult situation. The self-compassion group also demonstrated higher levels of feeling safe after the exercise, as measured by heart rate monitors.

It Is Selfish

I remember sitting on an airplane years ago with Jackson, then five years old. Shortly before takeoff, the flight attendant stopped by our seats to remind me, in the event of a cabin pressure emergency, to put my oxygen mask on first, before securing Jackson's. When she was safely out of earshot, Jackson turned to me with distress in his eyes. "Mom, you wouldn't really put your mask on *first*, would you?" I responded that although I loved him more than anything in the world, if I didn't put my oxygen mask on first, I would not be able to help him with his oxygen mask, and then both of us would be in danger. The best way for me to take care of him was to first take care of myself.

Many people conflate self-compassion with selfishness. Once again, research shows the opposite is true. Professors at the University of Texas at Austin recruited more than one hundred couples who'd been in a romantic relationship for a year or longer.[3] They found that self-compassionate individuals were described by their partners as being more caring, accepting, and respectful than their self-critical counterparts, who were described as being more detached, aggressive, and controlling.

Our body understands this truth: our heart, the single most important muscle in our body, pumps blood to itself first before sending blood to the rest of the body. Far from being selfish, it is both wise and necessary to learn to take care of ourselves. When we are able to give ourselves care and support and meet our own needs, we have more emotional resources available to help others.

It Is Self-indulgent

Another misconception is that self-compassion will make us self-indulgent slackers or couch potatoes who eat Twinkies all day long and never exercise. This couldn't be further from the truth. Research shows that self-compassionate people have healthier behaviors than non-self-compassionate people in terms of getting exercise, practicing safer sex, and eating healthfully.

The study of dieters discussed in chapter 5 reveals that self-compassion releases us from the shame and self-judgment that often undermine our best intentions to make healthy choices. When we care about ourselves, we are more likely to take care of ourselves.

> *When we care about ourselves, we are*
> *more likely to take care of ourselves.*

It Undermines Responsibility and Integrity

Some people mistakenly believe that self-compassion lets us evade responsibility and ignore the consequences of our actions because we'll just "forgive" ourselves. Far from letting ourselves off the hook, self-compassion creates a place of safety where we are able to squarely face our negative qualities without undermining our self-worth. We can reflect on them and objectively evaluate why they exist. This makes us better equipped to evaluate and learn from our mistakes and to make amends.

For example, researchers at the University of California, Berkeley, asked students to recall a recent action they felt guilty about—such as cheating on an exam, lying to a romantic partner, or saying something harmful.[4] Next, each student received one of three instructions: (1) write to themselves for three minutes from the perspective of a compassionate and understanding friend; (2) write about their positive qualities; or (3) write about a hobby they enjoyed. Later, the students were interviewed.

Students who wrote to themselves from the perspective of a compassionate friend were more motivated to apologize for their actions and more committed to not repeating their behavior. By acknowledging our failures with compassion, we are able to learn from our mistakes and take responsibility for them.

Self-compassion Is Weak

A final pervasive misgiving is that self-compassion will make us weak or passive. To the contrary, self-compassion is one of our most powerful sources of strength and resilience during hard times. Research shows that soldiers returning from Afghanistan who were taught self-compassion—to mindfully acknowledge their anxiety and fear and to bring kindness toward themselves in the face of it—had lower levels of PTSD.[5]

Similarly, David Sbarra and his colleagues at the University of Arizona examined whether self-compassion helps determine how well people adjust to another form of trauma: divorce.[6] The researchers found that participants who displayed more self-compassion when talking about their breakup were healthier and happier, and that this effect persisted nine months later. In short, they were more resilient.

The Three Elements of Self-Compassion

The best way to cultivate this valuable resource is to understand its three core elements as articulated by Kristin Neff: mindfulness, kindness, and common humanity.

1. **Mindfulness.** We need to be aware of pain before we can heal it. We understand this intuitively when it comes to physical pain. But facing mental or emotional pain is not easy, as many distractions exist to lure our consciousness away from what we fear or dislike. Mindfulness provides the non-judgmental "witness state" of consciousness that helps us see our pain clearly and *choose* to comfort and soothe it instead of succumbing to ingrained reactions of shame or avoidance.

2. **Kindness.** Kindness is the process of actively soothing ourselves: offering support and care when we are in pain. Importantly, we're not soothing ourselves to make the pain go away. We're soothing ourselves *because* we are in pain. When things go wrong, we often try to suppress the pain, berate ourselves, or leap into problem-solving mode. But once again: imagine how you might support a friend who is suffering. Would you tell your friend to forget about it? Would you call your friend an "idiot"? Would you start barking out orders and instructions? Or would you offer your friend kindness, let them know you care—that no matter what happened or what will result from it, you love them?

3. **Common humanity.** Recognizing our common humanity reminds us that we are not alone in our suffering. Our belief that this is "my" personal problem or that we are the "only one" suffering isolates and separates us. Common humanity helps us recognize that other people also get divorced or have sick children or get stuck in traffic. Self-compassion helps us reframe our situation in light of our shared human experience. When we recognize our common humanity and don't take things so personally, we experience a greater sense of connection, comfort, and calm.

The Pink Ribbon

When I began working with Samantha, she was a single mother recently diagnosed with breast cancer. Facing double mastectomy, her tremendous anxiety about the surgery, her appearance, the possibility of cancer recurrence, and the potential medical bills nearly overwhelmed her. But greater still was her worry for her daughters' future—April and Heather, ages fourteen and eleven. With Samantha's parents quite elderly and no father in the picture, Samantha worried how she could possibly handle this on her own.

Over and over we practiced the three elements of self-compassion. Mindful of her fear and grief, she acknowledged them instead of pushing them away—allowing the sadness, the worry, and the pain. She was able to gently touch her pain with kindness, closing her eyes and saying to herself: *I'm here. I'm not going anywhere. I love you and I'm with you through all of this.*

We also worked on expanding her awareness of her common humanity, opening to the millions of women who were facing breast cancer at that very moment. Samantha imagined how it would feel if she could walk up to each of them and give them a hug, and how she would feel being held in their compassionate embrace.

Gradually, as she continued to practice, Samantha built the inner resilience to face her diagnosis, her treatment, and the uncertainty of what the future held. As she connected with other women, she felt a natural compassion for them, and she was able to begin to bring this same compassion to herself. Just as she wished for their healing, so too could she wish for her own.

The day before her surgery, she told me that every time she saw someone wearing a pink ribbon, she knew they were on her team rooting for her. She realized she was not alone in this journey.

Equally important, Samantha had harnessed a universal truth: she could be her own inner ally.

Like Samantha, we all face challenges, conflicts, and tragedies in life. Self-compassion not only comforts us during these difficult times, it also helps us grow resources to become a stronger, wiser version of ourselves. "Let me fall if I must fall. The one I will become will catch me," said the venerated eighteenth-century rabbi Baal Shem Tov. Falling is part of life. The key is to develop practices that help us respond to our falls with courage, compassion, and grace, just as Samantha did.

Why We Sometimes Feel Worse Before We Feel Better

When we practice self-compassion, strong and painful emotions may arise at first. This is understandable. Self-compassion takes us into the depths of our heart where we hold our most painful and tender memories and experiences. As we practice self-compassion, it can unveil these pains, allowing them to rise to the surface of our consciousness.

In their wonderful book, *The Mindful Self-Compassion Workbook*, psychologists Kristin Neff and Christopher Germer offer insight and reassurance about this phenomenon:

> Most of our hearts are hot with suffering accumulated over a lifetime. To function in our lives, we have needed to shut out stressful or painful experiences to protect ourselves. This means that when we open the door of our hearts and the fresh air of self-compassion flows in, old pain and fear is likely to come out.[7]

If this happens to you, remember that it's natural to feel these strong and painful emotions. It is important to keep offering yourself compassion, especially for the painful emotions that are arising. You can use your mindfulness to explore with openness and curiosity where you feel the emotions in your body. If the experience becomes too distressing, it is okay to simply pause and say to yourself: *This is really hard. It's time to rest and take a break. I can come back to this when I'm ready.*

Self-compassion is not a quick fix, and there is no need to push an overly intense experience. Self-compassion takes strength, courage, and faith. I encourage you to trust the process, and allow yourself to slowly let in more self-compassion, more kindness, a few degrees at a time. You can begin again in any moment.

PRACTICE   **Self-Compassion in Practice**

Call to mind a current challenge you are facing. Perhaps it is a struggle with one of your children. Or maybe you missed a deadline at work and are afraid of what your boss or colleagues will say. Or perhaps it is a difficulty with late-night eating. Choose one struggle that you want to work with.

Mindfulness: Please write down the situation as clearly and objectively as possible. Notice how you feel as you write about it. See if you can mindfully acknowledge your emotions and become aware of any accompanying body sensations (e.g. tightness in my throat, fear in my chest). Also, be aware how you may be judging yourself for what happened. Write down anything you notice.

Kindness: Write down some kind statements that you could make to yourself in the face of this situation. For example: "This is painful. I am here with you." "You are really worried about your son. This is scary for you." "It's okay to make mistakes, I am learning." "You are overeating because you feel lonely. I care about you." As you write these kind statements, you may want to pause and put your hand on your heart as a gesture of self-care.

Common humanity: Remind yourself how natural it is for hard times to arise, and for you to feel scared, or frustrated, or sad. Reflect on all the other people in the world who might be in a very similar situation right now. Write down your reflections. For example: "It is natural to feel sad after having an argument with my son. Many parents struggle with their children." As you connect in your mind and heart with others in your same situation, try sending them and yourself compassion and kindness. For example: "I love my son and I feel scared about his safety. I imagine many parents are scared about their children right now. I am sending compassion to myself and all parents."

GOLD NUGGET Pause and reflect on the highlights from this chapter and then choose one Gold Nugget you want to take with you and encode in your long-term memory. Write it down in your journal.

Sample Gold Nuggets:

- You can be your own inner ally.
- You are never alone in your suffering.
- Self-compassion is strong.

SIX PRACTICES
FOR TOUGH TIMES

Have you ever noticed that anyone
driving slower than you is an idiot, and anyone going
faster than you is a maniac?
GEORGE CARLIN

The mind is its own place, and in itself can make
a heaven of hell, a hell of heaven.
from *Paradise Lost* by **JOHN MILTON**

A couple years ago, I went to Bhutan to collaborate with the
executive director of the Gross National Happiness Index
project. As part of my trip, I was invited to a dinner with his
Royal Highness the Prince of Bhutan and many governmental
officials of the country. I entered the exquisitely decorated
dining room to find eight large, round tables, each alight with
candles and colorful flowers. I was told that each table hosted
an honorary guest from Bhutan to facilitate the dinner. I had
been assigned to the table with the head of military and police.

I'll admit, I was disappointed. And a wee bit judgmental.
Military? Police? I was a mindfulness and compassion researcher,

for heaven's sake. Why hadn't I been assigned to the minister of health or education or happiness?

Unsettled, I found my place next to the chief of police. We sat in silence for some time. Finally, with hesitation, I asked him to tell me about the military and police in Bhutan. With a welcoming smile and eyes bright, he said, "Police are seen as the parents, teachers, helpers, and protectors. They remind people of their values, of how to treat others—of who their best selves are."

He went on to share how he trains his officers in compassion. Then, more somberly, he said, "A police without compassion is a very dangerous thing."

My eyes filled with tears, touched by his wisdom and aware of how my preconceived ideas had created stress where none was needed, potentially blinding me to this beautiful moment.

We tend to think of stress as something that happens outside of ourselves; something that happens *to* us. But science is showing that it's not the stressors in our life, but how we *perceive* them that determines how much we suffer.

We may not have control over the challenges we face, but we do have choice in how we perceive and respond to them. As meditation teacher Satchidananda says, "You can't stop the waves, but you can learn how to surf."[1]

Below, we'll explore six specific mind-sets and practices, born from the heart of mindfulness, that can empower us to surf life's waves with greater skill and ease.

The Power of Acceptance:
What We Resist, Persists

In a popular story, a teacher walking outdoors with his students points to a very large boulder and says, "Students, do you see that boulder?" The students respond, "Yes, teacher, we see the boulder." The teacher asks, "And is the boulder heavy?" The students respond, "Oh, yes, teacher, very heavy." To which the teacher replies, "Not if you don't pick it up."

We inevitably encounter "boulders" throughout life. Whether they crash without warning or whether we knew, deep down, there was a rockslide waiting to happen, we have two options: we resist them, or we accept them.

One of the great paradoxes of mindfulness is that by accepting pain, we reduce our suffering. Our resistance to pain compounds and increases our suffering. Mindfulness teaches us how to accept the boulders of life.

> *One of the great paradoxes of mindfulness is that by accepting pain, we reduce our suffering.*

To be clear, acceptance isn't the same as passive resignation. Nor is it approval, indifference, or defeat. Acceptance means that we accept what is happening not because we like it, or don't care, or have given up—but because it already *is happening*. Acceptance means that we open our eyes and look straight at the boulder so we can see it clearly and determine how to respond effectively.

We all encounter pain in life, lose friends and family, get sick, grow old, and die. So do the people we love. Pain in life is inevitable. Suffering, on the other hand, is optional.

> *Pain in life is inevitable. Suffering, on the other hand, is optional.*

This notion that we can disentangle pain from suffering can be a mystifying idea. How is that possible? Think for a moment about our usual response to pain: we spend endless time and energy fighting the boulders in our life to get things just the way we want them. Then, have you noticed what happens? Just when we finally get the boulders lined up, wipe the sweat from our brow, and stroll down the seemingly clear path ahead . . . *bam*! We run straight into another boulder. Again, we sweat and struggle, push and pull, get it where we want it, and . . . *bam*!

What most of us fail to realize is that this is just the way life is. Even if we manage to twist and bend reality into the way we want it for a moment, in the next moment things change. This is one of the fundamental laws of nature: everything changes. When we resist this reality, we suffer.

Acceptance is the surprising antidote to suffering because it helps us *understand* our experience rather than drown in it. Acceptance shifts our relationship to what is happening and separates the pain that is inevitable from the suffering that is optional. In fact, how much we suffer in any given moment depends on how much we resist the pain. It comes down to a simple yet powerful equation I learned from meditation teacher Shinzen Young:

$$\textit{Suffering} = \textit{Pain} \times \textit{Resistance} \ (S = P \times R)^2$$

From a mathematical perspective, the result of any number multiplied by 0 is 0. Thus, if we have zero resistance to our pain, we have zero suffering. This doesn't mean that we don't still experience pain. It means *we have control over how much we suffer.*

For example, when we get stuck in traffic, we often become impatient and irritated, wanting the other cars to get out of our way. We also might get frustrated with ourselves, thinking, "Why did I take this route? Why didn't I check traffic before I left?" The *pain* of traffic gains power over us as we embroil ourselves in a fog of fury and self-judgment, adding boulder upon boulder to our *suffering*.

Imagine, on the other hand, that we accept the reality instead of compounding it with resistance, and free up our resources to face the challenge. Instead of fuming over the undeniable fact that we are now stuck in traffic, we can accept what is.

As we slow down our racing thoughts, perhaps we notice the sunshine filtering through the car window. Or perhaps we become aware of the other drivers and notice how frustrated they are, too, recognizing that from their point of view, *we* are the traffic slowing *them* down! We're all in the same boat.

Or perhaps we simply let our exhausted minds rest for a few minutes, giving ourselves much-needed breathing space, before we head into our task-packed day. We might even practice some deep breathing and feel our bodies begin to relax.

I don't mean to suggest that this is easy. And to be sure, there are many life events far more challenging than a simple traffic jam. But I have come to believe that even when faced with the end of life itself, we always have a choice in how we perceive a situation and how we respond to it. Resistance only begets more suffering. Acceptance brings peace and possibility.

By accepting what is, we put ourselves back in the driver's seat. As Frank Ostaseski, founder of Zen Hospice Project, beautifully puts it, "Acceptance is not resignation. It is an opening to possibility."[3]

PRACTICE Acceptance

Sit quietly and allow your body and mind to rest. Set an
intention to cultivate the power of acceptance. Bring
your *attention* into the present moment with an *attitude*
of kindness and curiosity. Intentionally bring to mind a
painful area of your life where it could help to practice less
resistance and greater acceptance.

How does your resistance manifest? Does it show up as
bursts of anger; self-defeating behavior; avoidance; physical
symptoms such as sleeping too much or too little, eating
too much or too little; or maybe by trying to control or
force things? With an attitude of kindness and curiosity, ask
yourself: *How is my resistance causing greater suffering to me
and/or to others?*

Now, gently direct your attention to what it would
feel like to practice greater acceptance of what is
happening—not because you want it to be happening, but
because it is already happening. Since it is already happening,
what might be the best way to deal with it? Spend a few
minutes noticing how this feels. And then, as you are ready,
take a deeper breath in and out and gently open your eyes.

Take a few minutes to write about your experience and
any insights you had. What did you notice? Does shifting
your relationship to the pain shift the amount of suffering
you experience?

The Power of Emotion Regulation

Stressful or difficult situations often cause what Dan Goleman, the author of *Emotional Intelligence*, calls the "amygdala hijack."[4] The amygdala—an almond-shaped mass located deep in our brain's temporal lobe—acts as our early-warning sentry. The moment something stressful happens, the amygdala sends a distress signal to our hypothalamus, which acts as the body's operating system and automatically triggers the fight-or-flight reactions of our sympathetic nervous system.

This biologically evolved process is great for those times when we step into the street and jump back to avoid an oncoming car, or when we need to catch that slippery smartphone before it falls in the toilet, but it's terrible for those times where even a modicum of logic would make the situation better instead of worse.

Learning to regulate your emotions is one of the best tools you have to prevent an amygdala hijack. This doesn't mean ignoring, suppressing, or otherwise getting rid of your emotions. In fact, science shows that suppressing emotions can backfire. Stanford University's James Gross found that people who tried to suppress a negative emotional experience failed to do so.[5] While these people thought they looked fine on the outside, inwardly their limbic system—the system that manages emotions—was just as active as the limbic systems of those who weren't trying to suppress their emotions—and in some cases, even more active.

Kevin Ochsner at Columbia University replicated these findings using fMRI to study the activity of the brain.[6] Bottom line: Trying not to feel something doesn't work, and in some cases even makes things worse.

If suppressing our emotions doesn't work, what's the best way to regulate them? The answer: to become aware of and label our emotions. We do this through *emotional tuning*.

Interestingly, we're wired to feel emotions before we know they exist. Yes, you read that correctly. There's no direct pathway between the emotional centers deep inside the middle brain and the biologically advanced outer cortex responsible for conscious thought and awareness. Instead, emotions travel directly from the middle brain to the body and from the body back into consciousness in the cortex.

How can we regulate our emotions if our cognitive brain is the last to know? With emotional tuning, we can train our brain to recognize our emotions by sensing and labeling them as they manifest in our body.

Research shows that when we loop in our cognitive brain in this simple, mindful way, we can interrupt and calm down an amygdala hijack.

Matthew Lieberman and David Creswell conducted a study with undergraduates at the University of California, Los Angeles, in which each student was placed in an MRI scanner and shown a variety of images with emotionally expressive faces.[7] Students were randomly asked to identify either the gender of the faces *or* the emotion being expressed by the faces. Lieberman and Creswell discovered an interesting pattern: there was a marked difference in brain reactions when students named the emotion expressed in the faces compared to when they named the gender.

When students named the emotion—such as anger, fear, excitement, happiness—their brain scans showed that the *amygdala calmed down*. By identifying and naming the emotions, these students put a brake on their emotional reactivity.

We call this process of mindfully identifying emotions "name it to tame it." All you need are a few words to describe emotions or sensations in the body indicative of emotions: for example, "I'm feeling scared," "my throat is tightening," or "I'm noticing tension in my shoulders."

This process of mental noting, or naming, activates our prefrontal cortex, which helps to reduce the spikes in our limbic system that cause our emotional reactivity, and strengthens the pathways between the body and the cortex. Emotional tuning gives us access to vital information about our feelings—both positive and negative—growing our capacity to consciously identify and learn from what we are feeling.

We also gain a potent moment of space between what's happening and our reaction to it, leading to one of our greatest allies in meeting challenges: *response flexibility*. Just by naming our emotions, we free ourselves from emotional reactivity and gain the flexibility to consciously choose from a wide array of skillful responses.

So, while we can't eliminate stress, we can, through repeated practice, train ourselves to identify and regulate our emotions, leading to greater clarity, wisdom, and happiness.

> > *While we can't eliminate stress, we can, through repeated practice, train ourselves to identify and regulate our emotions, leading to greater clarity, wisdom, and happiness.*

PRACTICE   **Emotion Regulation**

Allow your eyes to close and settle yourself into your body. Set an **intention** to deepen your capacity to regulate your emotions. Bring your **attention** into the present moment with an **attitude** of kindness and curiosity. Gently call to mind a stressful situation. Notice any emotions that arise in your body. Use the physical sensations you are noticing to help you identify and name what you are feeling. For example, do you notice that your jaw has clenched, your throat feels tight, your breathing has become more shallow? These are just some examples of how the body may manifest emotions.

Mentally note and then write down the emotion(s) you experience and the physical sensations that accompanied them. As you review your list, gently offer yourself the three reminders below. They are here for you to use now and in the future to help support you in becoming aware of and labeling your emotions:

1. **Remember that our emotions are here for a reason.** They often serve as a smoke alarm, letting us know about an impending fire. When we ignore or repress our emotions, it can lead to bigger problems.

2. **Remember that emotions have a limited time span, typically lasting for only thirty to ninety seconds.** Emotions arise, do their dance, and pass away, just like waves in the ocean. When we remember that this painful feeling will not last forever, it becomes more manageable to attend to.

3. **Remember to welcome all your emotions with an attitude of kindness and curiosity.** See if you can become interested in the felt experience in the body. For example, you may feel sadness as a tightening in your throat, or fear as a contraction in your belly. All emotions have a signature in the body. See if you can welcome the full spectrum of your emotions with kindness.

The Power of Shifting Perspective

Mindfulness practice allows us to shift perspective from our personal subjectivity to an impersonal objectivity. No longer immersed in the drama of our egocentric narrative, we can instead stand back and simply witness it.

As we learn to observe our thoughts, feelings, body sensations, and stories, we are no longer completely embedded in or fused with them. We begin to strengthen what psychiatrist Arthur Deikman refers to as "the observing self."[8]

When we do, we discover that "the *awareness* of sensations, thoughts, and feelings is different from the sensations, thoughts, and feelings themselves."[9]

This ability to shift from an egocentric perspective to a witnessing state increases our ability to see clearly and choose how we will move forward—key to our potential for learning and growth.

I saw this powerful shift in action when my grandpa, a brilliant mathematics professor, was suffering from osteoarthritis. He had always been the strong one in the family, the patriarch—knowing exactly how to solve any problem. Now he was in constant, debilitating pain. It was hard to see him suffering. I desperately wanted to help.

I asked if he'd be open to learning mindfulness practices as a way to manage the pain. In his unwavering humility, Grandpa responded with a wholehearted yes. And so, this eighty-year-old man allowed his twenty-nine-year-old granddaughter to teach him.

After weeks of practice, Grandpa shared how the mindfulness practices were helping him separate the sensation of physical pain from his awareness of it. And then he identified one of the most profound insights about mindfulness: "The part of me that sees the pain is not the part of me that is in pain. My awareness of the pain is not in pain."

This is a key distinction, and it's not only true of physical pain. For example, if I am aware of sadness, my *awareness* isn't sad. Same with anxiety. Same with anger. Same with loneliness. No matter how bad you may feel inside, the part of you that knows how bad you feel is standing apart from it. This is the part of you that can help you get through.

Mindfulness practice helps us begin to see that our experience is not *all* of who we are. Our experience is just one star in the night sky. Our awareness is the *entire* sky.

From this perspective, the pain, the sadness, the fear, become less scary. There is no need to flee, deny, suppress, or fight our experience. We can learn to take refuge in our awareness and simply witness the sensations of pain, sadness, or fear as stars in the sky, not defining all of who we are.

> › *Mindfulness practice helps us begin to see that our experience is not **all** of who we are. Our experience is just one star in the night sky. Our awareness is the* entire *sky.*

Although mindfulness practice didn't "cure" Grandpa's pain, it shifted his relationship to it. And as his relationship to the pain shifted, it opened up space for him to re-engage in life.

Grandpa and I decided to write a paper about this shift in perspective, suggesting it was one of the key mechanisms through which mindfulness had its transformative effects. This paper, published in the *Journal of Clinical Psychology*, was one of two most cited papers that year and to this day is my most referenced scholarly article.[10]

All of us can think of a time in our lives when we were caught in our own perspective and could have benefited from this ability to take a more objective perspective. Mindfulness helps us practice this skill so that it grows and becomes a resource to support us during difficult times. Below is a simple yet powerful practice to strengthen this resource.

PRACTICE Shifting Perspective

For this practice, you'll need paper and pen beside you. Sit quietly and allow your body and mind to rest. Set an *intention* to cultivate the power of shifting perspective. Bring your *attention* into the present moment with an *attitude* of kindness and curiosity. Gently call to mind a difficult situation you are experiencing with another person. Set a timer for four minutes and write down your thoughts and feelings about the situation.

When the timer rings, pause, return your attention to your body and breath, and notice how you feel.

Again, set the timer for four minutes. This time, write from the perspective of the person you are having the difficulty with. Try to sense this person's thoughts, emotions, perspective, and experience.

When the timer rings, pause, return your attention to your body and breath, and notice how you feel.

Finally, invite a wise being to join you. This could be your wisest, highest self, a dear friend, a teacher or therapist, even the Virgin Mary or the Dalai Lama. With your eyes closed, imagine this wise being sitting close by you, perhaps even with an arm around you, supporting you. Feel their strength, wisdom, and compassion. Invite their guidance in this difficult situation.

How might they respond? What is their perspective? Gently open your eyes, set your timer for four minutes, and write about this situation from the lens of the wise being.

When the timer rings, pause, return your attention to your body and breath, and notice how you feel.

Know that this wisdom, this capacity to shift perspective, is always here inside of you, available in any moment.

The Power of Compassion to Ease "Empathy Distress"

Empathy is our inherent ability to feel what another person is feeling. I hope that you were able to experience it in the practice above. We have this capacity thanks to an extraordinary system in our brains comprised of what are called mirror neurons.

These brain cells were discovered in the 1990s by a group of neuroscientists directed by Giacomo Rizzolatti, from the University of Parma (Italy). As Rizzolatti describes them, mirror neurons "allow us to understand other people's mind, not only through conceptual reasoning but through imitation. Feeling, not thinking."[11]

Even though the words are sometimes used interchangeably, empathy and compassion are not the same thing. Empathy is the ability to feel what someone is feeling. Compassion is the desire to help that person.

Scientists are learning that if empathy is not paired with compassion, it can lead to some negative consequences. When we view someone in pain, our mirror neurons cause the areas of the brain responsible for pain to become activated in our own brain. This can lead to empathic distress, which can overwhelm us. However, the answer is not to shut ourselves off and become emotionally numb.

The true power of empathy is as a gateway to compassion: the desire to help and alleviate the suffering of another. Recent research from the Max Planck Institute of Human Cognitive and Brain Sciences in Germany demonstrates that in the presence of another person's suffering, compassion registers as a positive emotion in our brain, whereas empathy registers as pain.[12] Brain scans show that compassion practice, unlike empathy, strengthens the brain's circuitry for joy and boosts the connections between the prefrontal cortex (the seat of our higher-order reasoning) and the emotional center of the brain, thereby activating feelings of love, affiliation, and connection.[13]

Thus, compassion can counteract empathy distress. While empathy helps us understand the pain of another person, compassion opens the possibility for us to do something positive about it by stimulating our desire to help.

> *While empathy helps us understand the*
> *pain of another person, compassion opens*
> *the possibility for us to do something positive*
> *about it by stimulating our desire to help.*

To use our natural empathic response as a gateway to compassion, we can focus our attention on the love and care we feel for someone in pain instead of focusing solely on the person's pain. This lights up our brain's reward centers and enhances our ability to offer our deepest resources, without creating added distress in ourselves. Rather, as we shift from empathy to compassion, we create feelings of connection and care, turning negative into positive.

It seems like emotional alchemy. But our brains are built to do this. And with practice, we can transform pain again and again.

PRACTICE **Compassion**

Sit quietly and allow your body and mind to rest. Set an *intention* to cultivate the power of compassion. Bring your *attention* into the present moment with an *attitude* of kindness and curiosity. Reflect on someone in your life who is going through a tough time. Take a couple of moments to feel this person's pain, allowing your natural empathy to arise. Notice how this feels in the body. Perhaps a lump in your throat, or tears, or tightness in your body.

Now, begin to transform your feelings of empathy into compassion by dropping beneath the pain, asking, "Why do I feel this pain?" As you do this you will mostly likely recognize, "It is because I love and care for this person."

Spend several minutes going deeper into feeling your love for them. Feel your genuine caring and your desire to help. Focus all of your attention on your heart's desire for this person's suffering to pass. What might you say to this person to express your compassion, your caring? Perhaps, "I care about you. I care about your pain. May it pass quickly. May you be well."

Once you have completed this practice, notice if you feel more depleted or more resourced, and perhaps write down one action you want to take to help support your friend who is suffering. Write down any other insights in your notebook.

The Power of Radical Responsibility

As we become more compassionate toward others and toward ourselves, we deepen our capacity to take *radical responsibility* for all of our actions, thoughts, feelings, and behaviors.

Taking responsibility without falling into a pit of shame, defeat, or self-judgment is one of the essential skills for effectively responding to difficult situations.

As we've learned, shame hijacks our amygdala, which triggers our stress responses and shuts down our capacity to act with wisdom and compassion. When that happens, we often run from responsibility, denying that there's anything we could do, or rationalizing what we did do.

It's understandable. Our own shame and self-blame make it too painful to acknowledge our mistakes. But this lack of responsibility keeps us stuck in repeating the same unhealthy behaviors again and again.

Every situation arises from numerous causes, conditions, interactions, timing, and factors we may know only in hindsight—or may never know. Paradoxically, only once we release ourselves from the grip of shame can we harness our power to take responsibility for our situation. It's our shame that locks us into repeating mistakes.

So, how do we see our unhealthy behaviors clearly and take responsibility for them, without judging ourselves? We do it by applying *healthy discernment* instead of *toxic shame*. Discernment evaluates things clearly but resists labeling them as good or bad.

> *It's our shame that locks us into repeating mistakes.*

Take poison as an example. A judgmental view of poison is that it will kill you; therefore, poison is "bad." A discerning view of poison is that it will kill you if ingested in a specific quantity. Mold, for instance, can be poisonous, but it is also life-saving at the right doses, when the mold is penicillin. When we discern instead of judge, we open up possibilities and allow ourselves flexibility to respond.

As we cultivate our capacity to discern, we improve our ability to see our habit patterns that lead us to act in certain ways. We begin to see the powerful neural superhighways of thoughts, emotions, and behaviors we've practiced for a lifetime: *Oh. This is what I do when I feel lonely. This is how I act when I'm angry. This is what I say when I'm trying to cover my hurt/shame/worry.* And so on. Healthy discernment lets us see these superhighways and choose another path: we can take radical responsibility for ourselves and for what we do next.

Mindfulness gives us the capacity to recognize parts of ourselves we're ashamed of. Compassion gives us the courage to wade through these dark places with wisdom and love. This compassionate clarity gives us the courage to take radical responsibility, allowing us to accept what has happened without shame, and then take steps to heal.

> *Mindfulness gives us the capacity to recognize parts of ourselves we're ashamed of. Compassion gives us the courage to wade through these dark places with wisdom and love.*

PRACTICE   Radical Responsibility

Sit quietly and allow your body and mind to rest. Set an *intention* to cultivate the power of radical responsibility. Bring your *attention* into the present moment with an *attitude* of kindness and curiosity. Reflect on a situation that brings up self-blame: something you've done that is hard for you to accept or forgive.

See if you can sense that there have been certain conditions in your life that may have been outside of your control or awareness, or that you didn't sign on for, that have led you to this place. See how your fears, confusions, pain, and reactivity have been shaped by multiple factors, from your life experiences and personal history to cultural conditioning and even genetics. See if you can open to the possibility that some aspects of this situation are part of the human condition. See if you can see this part of yourself and your life clearly and with compassion. Can you hold yourself accountable without blaming yourself?

As you begin to own this part of you and take responsibility for it, can you make a commitment toward one small way you can respond to the situation differently in the future? Take a couple minutes to write down any insights or commitments in your journal.

The Power of Forgiveness

Forgiveness is perhaps the most challenging of all the resources available to us—and the most transformational. Forgiveness requires us to integrate all of the skills we've learned thus far: acceptance, emotion regulation, shifting perspectives, compassion, and radical responsibility. As we begin to face the challenges of life with mindfulness and compassion, we begin to recognize our shared humanity. In doing so, we strengthen our capacity to forgive ourselves and others.

Forgiveness does not ignore the truth of our own or others' suffering. It is a courageous practice requiring us to honestly face our own shadows and the shadows that exist in others. We are not the only ones who struggle, who are in pain, who have caused pain to others, who have done things we're ashamed of, who've failed to be our best selves.

This collective pain creates calcifications around our heart and can block our capacity to fully love. Forgiveness gives us the power to dissolve these petrified emotional barriers and frees us to find happiness. As the thirteenth-century poet Rumi puts it, "Your task is not to seek for love, but merely to seek and find all the barriers within yourself that you have built against it."[14]

Forgiveness gives us a powerful path to reduce our own suffering and bring greater dignity and harmony to our life. It opens our future by liberating it from burdens of the past. While forgiveness can be quite challenging, only forgiveness can bring about the peace we long for within ourselves and among humankind.

There is a story of two ex-prisoners of war reuniting many years after their release. The first asks, "Have you forgiven your captors yet?" The second man answers, "No, never." "Well then," replies the first, "they still have you in prison."

Forgiveness fundamentally serves our own well-being. In fact, research shows that forgiveness has significant health benefits. Fred Luskin, founder of the Stanford University Forgiveness Project, has demonstrated with his colleagues that forgiveness reduces anger, depression, and stress and leads to greater feelings of optimism, hope, compassion, and self-confidence. It also benefits our physical health by enhancing our immune system and reducing cardiovascular disease and chronic pain.[15]

Forgiveness brings us back to the ground of love whenever we are lost. It frees us from our past, restores dignity, and opens us to life. But forgiveness doesn't happen overnight. It is a process that requires commitment and courage. Most of all, forgiveness takes practice.

PRACTICE   Forgiveness Meditation

I learned the following practice[16], one of the most powerful I've experienced, from meditation teacher Jack Kornfield while sitting my first month-long meditation retreat. It opened, stretched, and tenderized my heart. The version offered below was adapted from the practice he taught me.

Sit quietly and allow your body and mind to rest. Set an *intention* to cultivate the power of forgiveness. Bring your *attention* into the present moment with an *attitude* of kindness and curiosity. Rest your awareness in your body and on your breath flowing in and out. Let your body and mind relax, perhaps softening 5 percent more, letting go of any obvious tension.

Breathing gently into the area of your heart, invite in your sincere intention to release the barriers you have erected and the burdens of your past. It might be helpful to place a hand on your heart, to feel your own loving support.

As you are ready, begin reciting the following words:

Forgiveness of others: Reflect on the many ways you have hurt others out of your pain, fear, anger, and confusion. Let yourself remember one specific incident. Allow any images and emotions that accompany the memory to surface. Open yourself to the sorrow and the regret. When you are ready, silently ask for forgiveness: *I ask for your forgiveness, I ask for your forgiveness. Please forgive me.*

Forgiveness for yourself: Reflect on the ways you have harmed yourself, betrayed yourself, or abandoned yourself. Choose one specific incident, and allow yourself to feel the sorrow you have carried from this. Feel how precious this life is. As you are ready, begin to silently repeat: *I forgive myself, I forgive myself.* Or, *May I forgive myself.*

Forgiveness for those who have hurt or harmed you: Reflect on the ways you have been hurt, betrayed, or abandoned by others. Choose one person or experience you want to begin to forgive. Feel the sorrow and pain you have carried from this past and sense that you can begin to release the burden of this pain. Silently repeat to yourself: *To the extent that I am ready, I offer you forgiveness. I forgive you.* Or, *May I forgive you.*

Once you have completed these three directions of forgiveness, rest quietly with your attention on your heart. This is a powerful practice that can deeply stir emotions. Welcome everything with kindness. Trust that you are going at the right pace. Forgiveness cannot be forced or rushed. With continued gentle practice, your heart will heal and release the burdens of the past as it is ready.

Out beyond ideas of wrongdoing and rightdoing
there is a field. I'll meet you there.
When the soul lies down in that grass,
the world is too full to talk about.
Ideas, language, even the phrase *each other*
doesn't make any sense.   *RUMI*

GOLD NUGGET   Pause and reflect on the highlights from
this chapter and choose one Gold Nugget you want to take
with you and encode in your long-term memory. Write this
down in your journal.

Sample Gold Nuggets:

- Empathy can lead to activation of pain centers
  in the brain; compassion leads to activation
  of positive reward centers in the brain.
- Suffering = Pain × Resistance
- Shame locks us into repeating mistakes.
- Forgiveness is not about condoning someone's
  behavior; it is about freeing our own hearts by
  releasing the burden of anger and resentment.

PART 3

Growing the Good in Ourselves and in Our World

PRIMING THE MIND FOR JOY

Seven Practices

Everything has beauty, but not everyone sees it.
CONFUCIUS

One January morning at rush hour, in an arcade outside a Washington, DC, subway station, a youthful man in jeans, t-shirt, and baseball cap opened the instrument case he carried and took out a violin. He placed the case on the ground in the position universally understood to solicit donations, and started to play.

The man played for forty-three minutes as commuters streamed past. Just another day in the life of an enterprising artist and time-pressed commuters, you might say. And, in a way, it was.

But this wasn't just any struggling busker, playing valiantly away on a worn fiddle. It was internationally renowned violinist Joshua Bell. His performance included some of the most beautiful and difficult classical music written for the violin. And the fiddle was a 1713 Stradivarius made by the peerless Antonio Stradivari at the height of his artisanal powers, reportedly purchased by Bell for around $3.5 million.

What happened next in this experiment has become well known since this story went viral on the internet, and the original account in the *Washington Post* garnered a Pulitzer Prize.[1] Of the 1,097 people who passed Bell that morning, just seven actually stopped to listen for a minute or more. And his take? $32.17.

The nearby newsstand selling Lotto tickets got more attention than the free concert being offered by a virtuoso who, days earlier, had played to a full house where listeners paid $100 for a ticket.

This experiment and its outcome pose important questions: How often do we miss the beauty directly in front of us? Are we in such a rush, living on automatic pilot, that there is no time left for joy?[2]

The magic of mindfulness is that it not only aids us in difficult times, but it also magnifies life's inherent joy.

> > *The magic of mindfulness is that it not only aids us in difficult times, but it also magnifies life's inherent joy.*

Thus far we've focused on learning practices and growing resources to help us face the challenges of life. If we stopped here and simply practiced what we've learned, we'd all be better equipped to survive life's trials. But surviving isn't thriving. So many of us have lost touch with the simple joys, the everyday magic that makes life meaningful.

In fact, according to the 2017 Harris Poll Happiness Index, only one in three Americans reported being very happy.[3]

This is troubling, especially since research shows that being happier makes us healthier, more successful, and better citizens.

Professors Julia Boehm and Sonja Lyubomirsky have conducted numerous studies comparing people with varying levels of happiness. Time and again the research shows that "compared with their less happy peers, happy people earn more money, display superior performance, and perform more helpful acts." Happy people also live longer, stay married longer, have fewer illnesses, and are more resilient.[4]

The good news is that you can harness the power of happiness through mindfulness. In this chapter, you will learn specific practices that can sculpt and strengthen your neural circuits and increase your happiness setpoint—your individual innate happiness level, as we discussed in chapter 1. The first step is understanding why happiness is often elusive.

Elusive Elation: Why Being Happy Isn't Easy

One major reason why happiness is so elusive is that we're surprisingly poor predictors of what makes us happy. For example, we may think that a vacation, more money, having the "perfect" body, or owning our dream house will make us happy. But more often than not, we're wrong. Marketers have made billions from our poor guesses.

Nobel Prize winner Daniel Kahneman refers to this as "poor affective forecasting." Decades of research have shown that changing our external circumstances doesn't make us happier. As author Barbara De Angelis writes, "It's not rearranging things on the outside of your life that is going to make a permanent impact. It's rearranging things on the inside."[5] Luckily, as we've learned, we can restructure our internal landscape through repeated practice—as you will do later in this chapter with practices that can increase and deepen your happiness.

A second reason happiness is often elusive is because evolution has installed in our brain what psychologists refer to as a *negativity bias*. This describes the human tendency to focus more on the negative than on the positive.

Over millions of years, our very survival depended on scanning our environment for danger. Our anxious ancestors who fretted and worried about what lurking predator might be causing the leaves nearby to rustle were the ones who survived. The mellow ones who wanted to pet the pretty lion didn't last long enough to pass on their genes.

While our forebears' negativity bias was beneficial in the face of rampant physical danger, it wreaks havoc on us today by creating an unbalanced focus on the negative. Often we gloss over positive experiences or miss them entirely. For example, when you get an annual review at work, what do you remember most—the five points of praise, or the one criticism?

As psychologist Rick Hanson says, "The brain is like Velcro for bad experiences and Teflon for good ones."[6] This has been well documented: painful and traumatic experiences can become so deeply seared into our memory that they overwhelm our entire lives, while positive experiences just sort of slip away.

What's the antidote? Mindfulness. We have learned how mindfulness, and the practices that grow out of it, can help us relate to trauma and pain in healthier, more adaptive ways. Now we will learn how mindfulness can help us *install* positive experiences in the brain, raise our happiness setpoint, balance our negativity bias, and prime ourselves to truly appreciate and remember the full beauty of life.

From States to Traits: Turning Positive Experiences into Lasting Strengths

Mindfulness practice paves new pathways in our brain that lead to greater happiness by helping us pause and fully experience positive moments. By intentionally weaving these experiences into the fabric of our mind, we solidify positive experiences into building blocks of happiness instead of fleeting moments that vanish before our eyes. Mindfulness helps us train the mind to better attend to and remember the positive.

Research shows that just having an experience does not translate into actual learning. Our brain requires more than a fleeting experience to turn information from a state into a trait. To cultivate greater happiness, joy, or gratitude, we can use the Intention, Attention, Attitude model of mindfulness:

- **Intention:** Previously I noted research showing that simply setting an intention to be happy actually made people happier. When we experience joy, gratitude, or any positive emotion, setting our intention to remember it helps us install the positive emotion and experience into our long-term memory, making it a permanent building block for happiness.

- **Attention:** To turn a positive experience into a neuropathway of happiness, focus on it for at least twenty seconds, or approximately three deep breaths. That's how long we need to focus in order to install the experience in our long-term memory so that it becomes part of our neurochemical soup.[7]

- **Attitude:** The more vivid you make the experience, the more ingrained it becomes in your permanent

memory. The mindful attitudes of kindness and
curiosity help you welcome all of your senses, noting
what you see, smell, hear, touch, and taste. Each
detail acts as a tiny hook that morphs our brain
from Teflon into Velcro for positive experiences.

As you use your intention, attention, and attitude to install
positive experiences into your memory, you re-engineer your
brain to counteract evolution's negativity bias.

What's more: you don't have to wait for positive experiences
to serendipitously occur in order to deepen your happiness.
Mindfulness helps us become more attuned to joyous times *and*
it helps us actively cultivate them.

Below are seven practices that explicitly cultivate positive
emotions, enhance inner resources, and grow our happiness.

1. Smiling Meditation

Peace activist and meditation teacher Thich Nhat Hanh reminds
us of the power of smiling.[8] He invites us to bring a slight but
real smile to our lips while we are meditating and while we are
going about our day. The salutary benefits of a smile have been
confirmed by science, showing that a smile sends a biochemical
message to our nervous systems that it is safe to relax the flight-
fight-or-freeze response.[9]

2. Gratitude

The virtue of gratitude has been extolled throughout history
and across cultures. As German theologian Meister Eckhart
observed: "If the only prayer you ever say in your entire life is
'thank you,' it will be enough."

Marcy, 53, had faced cancer, enduring eight months of difficult treatment. She shared that her gratitude practice supported

her through it: "Each night at bedtime, I thought of three things I was grateful for. It could be the delicious dinner that my husband had prepared, for which I fortunately had an appetite. Or the nurse who gently patted my back during a treatment. Or my cozy night-cap that kept my bald head warm. When I felt scared—which was a lot—I focused on how grateful I was to have access to the most current and effective treatments. This practice would shift me from fear and isolation straight into gratitude, often to the point of tears. On many long nights, counting my blessings helped comfort me and find calmness and sleep."

Across hundreds of studies, scientists have demonstrated the link between gratitude and heightened levels of positive emotions. It is the foundation of well-being and the source of myriad benefits, including decreased depression,[10] increased resilience,[11] improved sleep,[12] decreased risk of cardiovascular disease,[13] and better, stronger relationships (including romantic ones).[14]

An attitude of gratitude has also been shown to improve the workplace. Grateful employees perform their jobs more effectively, feel more satisfied at work, and show more respect toward their coworkers. Research links gratitude with broadening our modes of thinking, creativity, and perspective-taking.[15]

How does it achieve all of these positives? Gratitude helps us pause and take in the good. Often, we're so preoccupied with the stressors in our lives that we miss the beauty surrounding us.

Intentionally directing our attention to what we are grateful for helps us recognize these positive experiences, instead of allowing them to slip by unnoticed. And there's a ripple effect: when we feel grateful, we're more likely in turn to extend that positive energy toward others, who then have an opportunity to experience, absorb, and share happiness. As renowned author Arianna Huffington beautifully puts it, "Living in a state of gratitude is the gateway to grace."[16]

PRACTICE Cultivating
an Attitude of Gratitude

Research has identified specific practices that strengthen
gratitude and can greatly increase our happiness and positive
mood.

Gratitude letter. Write a letter to someone for whom you feel
grateful, perhaps someone to whom you have not expressed
the extent of your gratitude. Reflect on concrete details you are
grateful for in this person. Describe specific moments. Again,
the more you include sensory details and particulars, the more
you will receive the benefits of gratitude—and the more your
letter will help the person receiving it feel and appreciate your
gratitude. You will be sharing the power of cementing positive
memories not only in your own mind, but in someone else's
mind as well.

"Three good things." In several similar but separate studies on
the use of gratitude, participants spent five to ten minutes at
the end of each day writing in detail about three things, large
or small, that went well that day. This resulted in increased
happiness as well as enhanced well-being, better access to
positive memories, reduced stress, and a greater sense of
flourishing in life.[17] If you try this practice, make sure you
include details that activate your senses. What did you
see, hear, smell, taste, or feel? Each sensory detail helps the
memory stick in the brain. Write in your journal what you
noticed.

3. Generosity

The University of Notre Dame is home to the Science of Generosity initiative. The project defines generosity as "giving good things to others freely and abundantly."[18] Typically, we think of generosity as something we do for someone else. But research shows that being generous increases our own happiness—in fact, there is a neural link between generosity and happiness.

Professor Soyoung Park and his colleagues took brain scans of people while asking them to imagine committing a generous act. Immediately after deciding to act selflessly, the parts of the brain responsible for reward and pleasure became active. What's more, people reported feeling happier following the study.[19]

We refer to this phenomenon as altruism or *enlightened selfishness*. It feels good to be generous because we are hardwired for it. Throughout evolution, groups and communities with stronger bonds were the most successful and the ones that survived. Generosity is what deepens these bonds. Nature selected the genes that predispose us to practice generosity, which leads to stronger, more connected communities.

This idea that we are born to be generous seems in stark contrast to conventional wisdom equating human nature with selfishness and self-preservation. A cartoon I recently saw captured this notion. It showed two photographers on safari in Africa, in open grassland. A lion appears. Both photographers freeze, terrified. One slowly bends down to lace up his shoes, and the other one says, "There's no way you can outrun a lion." To which the first photographer replies, "As long as I can outrun you!"

While humans undoubtedly have a propensity for self-interest, research has revealed the currents of generosity also run deep.

Research shows that generosity is good for us. It is significantly associated with happiness, physical health, and well-being. In their book *The Paradox of Generosity*, Christian Smith and

Hilary Davidson find that happy people report volunteering 5.8 hours of their time per month compared to less happy people, who average only 0.6 hours per month.[20]

The generosity-happiness link is an upward spiral: giving to others yields positive emotions, positive emotions further inspire generosity, and so on.

This is true in the workplace as well. Research shows that teams with high generosity not only create a culture of kindness and giving, but also a culture of enhanced productivity.

Sadly, even though generosity is healthy for us and creates more success in the workplace, the percentage of people who volunteer each year has been steadily decreasing over the past decade in the United States and the United Kingdom.[21] We have the capacity to be generous, but we don't always practice it.

PRACTICE   Cultivating Generosity

One easy, effective practice to strengthen generosity in ourselves and in society as a whole is to commit to one random act of kindness each day. Set an intention to look for one new way each day that you can give. These acts of kindness can be quite simple—for example, buying a cup of coffee for a stranger, giving up a parking space to another driver, or surprising someone with flowers. Write in your journal what you notice about these experiences, remembering to describe the sensory details and the emotions you feel.

---

4. See the Good in Others

Imagine walking into a room where there was someone who really disliked you. This person knows all of your flaws, mistakes, and vulnerabilities. They not only see the worst in you, but they expect it of you. How might you feel? How might you act?

Now imagine walking into that same room where there is someone who sees the best in you, knows your talents, and believes in you. They are on your team, rooting for you. How might you feel? How might you act?

A landmark study by Robert Rosenthal and Lenore Jacobson demonstrated the benefits of seeing the good in others. Rosenthal and Jacobson told a group of teachers that certain students in their classes were likely to surge ahead of their fellow students, based on a test the researchers had administered. When retested at year's end, these "growth spurters" had indeed made much greater gains compared to their peers.[22]

But there was a catch: the "growth spurters" had been randomly selected by the researchers, and were not based on real test results. This fabrication had been relayed to the teachers. What, then, made the difference in their success? The expectation of the teacher. The teachers' belief in the students' ability actually resulted in true higher test scores at the end of the year.

Over the past fifty years, these profound findings have been replicated in other environments. Bottom line: If you seek to find the good in others, you are most likely to draw it out.

We can also learn to see the good in ourselves. We can learn to believe in ourselves, just like this six-year-old girl:

> A first-grade teacher is walking around the room and stops to look over the shoulder of a little girl, asking,

"So, what are you drawing, Lucy?" The little girl responds, "I'm drawing God." The teacher chuckles, "But no one knows what God looks like." Without missing a beat, Lucy responds, "They will in a minute."[23]

PRACTICE **Seeing the Good in Others**

To practice and grow the ability to see the good in others, set an intention to look for the good in one person for a week. You could choose your child, parent, partner, colleague, or yourself (for many of us, this is the advanced practice!). Commit to looking for the good in that person every day for a week. Write in your journal something you appreciate and admire about this person each day (e.g.: *I appreciate how my husband washed the dishes after dinner* or *I loved hearing my son laughing out loud in his room*). Notice what happens as you start to look for the good in others. How does this impact your feelings toward this person? How does it impact *their* behavior?

---

5. Empathic Joy (*Mudita*)

We often have the irrational mind-set that there's only so much good fortune to go around, so the more someone else has, the less there will be for us. We know this is logically untrue, but our scarcity mentality results in spates of envy. Thankfully, we can learn to find genuine happiness within ourselves by rejoicing in the happiness of others.

The practice of sharing in someone else's happiness is referred to as *mudita* in the Pali language. Interestingly, there is no equivalent word in the West. The closest would be "empathic joy."

As the Dalai Lama puts it, there are so many people in this world, it simply makes sense to make their happiness a source of our own. Then, our chances of experiencing joy are enhanced nearly eight billion to one—and those are very good odds.

A 57-year-old woman I worked with had recently endured a devastating divorce. She was struggling with the loss and felt an overwhelming loneliness. She shared how painful it was every time she saw a couple in love. She would well up with jealousy, which then would boil over into shame that she was feeling jealous.

We worked on practicing mudita. Every time she saw a couple in love, she would practice focusing on the joy they were experiencing and wishing that it continue, as well as wishing that she would find this kind of love in her own life.

After a while, she began to feel happy when she saw couples in love, genuinely able to wish them well and to see them as inspiration and signs of hope that she would love again. When we learn to celebrate others' happiness, we come to understand that happiness is not a limited commodity. Others' happiness doesn't lessen our chances, but actually brings the very happiness we seek into our lives.

PRACTICE **Cultivating Mudita**

The following practice helps us develop mudita. Sit comfortably with your eyes closed and silently reflect on your intention to find happiness in the happiness of others.

Next, call to mind someone you love who is having good fortune. It could be a dear friend who recently got pregnant after years of trying, or a dear colleague who received an award after much dedicated work. As you call the person to mind, picture their joy, their happiness. Then silently recite these phrases: "May your happiness continue." "I'm on your team, rooting for you." "May the joy in your life continue and grow." As you practice, you can offer the phrases to different people in your life, one by one.

It is natural to sometimes feel a pang of jealousy, or for difficult emotions to arise as you practice. Mudita is often called a purification practice, releasing negative thoughts that are inhibiting your happiness. When these thoughts or emotions arise, it is helpful to simply bring your mindfulness and compassion to them. See them clearly and respond with kindness: *Oh, sweetheart, you want to feel happy for your friend, but you also feel sad, because you were longing for that to happen to you.* No shame, no judgment, just seeing clearly with compassion.

As you do this practice repeatedly, you will naturally cleanse away negative reactions and begin to notice other people's joy more frequently, strengthening your capacity to celebrate it.

---

6. Awe and Wonder

Most of us can recall times when we've experienced the mysterious and complex emotion called awe. Maybe you've felt it while in the mountains or driving through rolling countryside, gazing at an unforgettable sunset, or watching animals in the wild. Perhaps you witnessed a simple gesture of love pass between an elderly couple, or attended the birth of a child. Awe shifts our attention away from our small sense of self and opens us to feeling that we are part of something greater. Awe inspires self-transcendence.

And awe is good for us. The latest research suggests that awe leads to a wide range of benefits, from happiness, improved relationships, and greater generosity to increased humility and critical thinking. It also leads to better health and helps stave off chronic disease. One study found that people who reported feeling more "awe, wonder, and amazement that day" had lower levels of inflammation and illness.[24]

Research also shows that awe can help us think critically and sharpen our brains.[25] It's when we feel inspired, not judged or shamed, that we find our peak performance. Using awe at work, in the classroom, and at home with our children is much more effective than criticism.

Finally, awe makes people kinder and more generous. For example, one study found that people with a greater tendency for awe were more generous in tasks assigned during the study, such as distributing raffle tickets between themselves and a stranger. And people who stood among awe-inspiring trees helped pick up more pens for an experimenter who had "accidentally" dropped them than people who stared up at a not-so-inspiring concrete building.[26]

Importantly, you don't need to take expensive vacations to exotic places or have deep religious experiences to feel awe. There are many ways to cultivate awe in everyday life. For example, research shows that simply witnessing a sunset or watching awe-inducing videos like a superb athletic or musical performance can improve your mood and well-being.

PRACTICE   **The Magical Morning Question**

To begin looking for awe and beauty in your daily life, try asking yourself one simple question when you wake each morning: "I wonder what unexpected and magical thing will happen today?" You'll be priming your mind to look for the mysterious, surprising, and miraculous, instead of its habitual pattern of looking for problems. This isn't some sort of affirmation that plants unrealistic expectations and sets you up for disappointment. It's a way to deliberately prime the mind for greater wonder and joy by fostering openness to the infinite possibilities that exist in every moment. Write in your journal about one surprising or magical thing you noticed today.

---

7. Kindness

"A side effect of kindness is happiness," writes David Hamilton, author of *The Five Side Effects of Kindness*.[27] Science is proving it. Research shows that lovingkindness meditations can enhance positive emotions, heighten life satisfaction, boost our personal resources, and serve as a buffer against depressive symptoms.

Results of Barbara Fredrickson's study at the University of North Carolina showed that just seven weeks of lovingkindness meditation increased people's daily experiences of positive emotions, which led to increases in personal resources (including increased purpose in life, social support, and decreased illness symptoms). These gains contributed to increased life satisfaction and decreased depressive symptoms.[28]

Lovingkindness meditation has also been proven to decrease bias toward others, decrease migraines, sharpen focus and attention, and instill a sense of feeling connected to others.[29] Cultivating kindness also leads to generosity. For example, web-based instruction in lovingkindness meditation for a total of about three-and-a-half hours (twenty sessions, ten minutes each) resulted in people feeling more relaxed and donating to charity at a higher rate than a comparison group that did light exercise and stretching for the same amount of time.[30]

PRACTICE **Lovingkindness Meditation**

Lovingkindness meditation is one of the most well-researched practices to strengthen kindness, happiness, and well-being. Below I offer an adapted version of the instructions developed by Sharon Salzberg, whose book *Lovingkindness* has been an inspiration and guide in my life.[31]

Begin by sitting or lying in a comfortable position. Let your mind and body be at ease. Place one hand on your heart and feel the sensation of your own touch. Rest your attention on your heartbeat and sense how your heart is taking care of you, sending oxygen and nutrients to the trillions of cells in your body. Simply rest here, let the heart take care of you.

When you are ready, call to mind a loved one, a dear friend, a child, a pet. Anyone who opens your heart. I often call to mind my grandfather, Ben. Whenever I think of him, my entire being smiles. As you bring this person to mind, feel your care and love for them. Imagine sending this lovingkindness to them using images and words. Whatever supports you in opening to a sense of this connection and this love.

Next, call to mind a person who loves you, who has supported and been kind to you. This person doesn't need to have been perfectly kind at all times. Remember, no one is perfect. But as best you can, choose someone who you feel has loved and supported you. Feel their care and their love for you. Imagine them with their arm around you wishing you well, sending you lovingkindness. And as you're ready, begin sending this same lovingkindness to yourself. It can be helpful to use images and words: consider saying to yourself, "May I be peaceful," and calling to mind an image of when you felt ease and peace; "May I be happy," and calling to mind an image of you happy and joyful; "May I be healthy" and imagine yourself healthy and strong; or "May I be filled with lovingkindness" and imagine love and kindness filling your being.

And as you are ready, offer these wishes to all beings. Send this love and kindness out in all directions to all beings and to the earth. Reflect that you are part of all beings . . . send the lovingkindness out with each exhale and breathe it in with each inhale.

As you are ready to draw the practice to a close, take a moment to allow the nourishment of this practice to sink in. Feel the wholesomeness of directing your attention in this way. It doesn't matter what you felt; what matters is that you are planting the seeds of kindness, pointing your mind in the direction of greater love.

———————

GOLD NUGGET   Pause and reflect on the highlights from this chapter and then choose one Gold Nugget you want to take with you and encode in your long-term memory. Write this down in your journal.

Sample Gold Nuggets:

- We can balance our negativity bias by engaging in practices that cultivate joy.
- We can install positive experiences into our long-term memory by focusing on them for three breaths.
- A side effect of kindness is happiness.
- Generosity is not only good for others; it is good for you.

9

EVERYDAY MAGIC

From Mindful Sex to Mindful Eating

There are only two ways to live your life.
One is as though nothing is a miracle.
The other is as though everything is a miracle.
ALBERT EINSTEIN

To see a World in a Grain of Sand
And a Heaven in a Wild Flower
Hold Infinity in the palm of your hand
And Eternity in an hour
WILLIAM BLAKE *Auguries of Innocence*

As we've been seeing, mindfulness is not just a meditation practice for when things get tough. *Mindfulness is a way of living, a way of being.* We can practice mindfulness in *every* moment of our lives, from making love to eating to working to parenting. The moment-to-moment availability of mindfulness is one of its greatest strengths, elevating it above the long list of stress management techniques.

> *Mindfulness is not just a meditation practice for when things get tough. **Mindfulness is a way of living, a way of being.***

I did not fully understand this until I was in my late twenties and my friend and mentor, the renowned author Ken Wilber, said something that stopped me in my tracks: "Shauna, you have kept your mindfulness practice completely cut off from your sexuality. They are not separate. They go hand in hand."

What?! My mindfulness practice, "up there" . . . part of sex, "down there?" This was revolutionary to me.

I hadn't had sex prior to my spinal fusion surgery at age seventeen. After the surgery (and the metal rod), it seemed horrifying to imagine anyone ever touching my body with desire. Not only was I in severe pain, but I also felt ashamed of my scars and my pale, emaciated body. When I finally had my first sexual experience in college with my boyfriend, I completely dissociated from my body, and for the few moments I was present, all I remember was the constant fear that I was doing it wrong.

Ken guided me to readings, teachers, and a path where I learned that mindfulness could be applied not only to sex, but to all dimensions of my life.

Mindfulness brings oxygen to our most intimate moments and to the most ordinary ones, breathing greater joy and vitality into our life. We begin to treat each moment as if it really matters, instead of as if we are on our way to something else. It helps us see the sacred in everything, transforming the mundane into magic. We stop waiting for life to begin and realize that this is it. Life is right now.

In this chapter you will learn how to bring the three elements of mindfulness—intention, attention and attitude—to everything you do by exploring how to apply them in five specific domains:

1. Mindful sex

2. Mindful decision-making

3. Mindfulness in the workplace

4. Mindful parenting

5. Mindful eating

Needless to say, the domains where mindfulness can be applied are infinite. But these five are particularly rich in opportunities to apply the fundamentals of mindfulness on a daily basis.

Mindful Sex

Take a moment to recall a pleasurable sexual experience you've had. Go on, really let yourself relive it, remembering the sights, sounds, touch, physical sensations, smells, and feelings. My guess is you were 100 percent present for your experience. Mindful sex happens when you're totally and completely immersed in the present moment.

We can learn to cultivate this state of presence with all of our sexual experiences—the extraordinary ones, the challenging ones, and the ones in between. By bringing mindfulness to sex and sexuality, we shine a light of gentle awareness on this topic that is deeply shrouded in cultural pressures and expectations.

Mindfulness gives us access to a more authentic, compassionate, and honest relationship to sex.

In fact, research shows that mindfulness practice has significant benefits on our sexual health and enjoyment. It increases arousal and awareness of pleasurable sensations during sex, as well as overall sexual satisfaction.[1] It also decreases cortisol, a stress hormone that prevents women from reaching orgasm.[2] Finally, groundbreaking research from University of California, San Francisco, showed that greater sexual activity with one's partner was associated with significantly longer telomeres. Telomeres are the caps at the end of chromosomes which protect our genes, our DNA. We need these protective caps to stay strong and healthy.[3]

Perhaps most importantly, research shows that mindfulness increases our connection with our body. So many of us go through the day living from the neck up, disconnected from our bodies. James Joyce captures this in his description of a character in *Ulysses*: "Mr. Duffy lived a short distance from his body." Can you relate? The good news is that mindfulness can help us reconnect with our body. It can even grow the area of the brain responsible for feeling our bodies.

For example, it turns out that size does matter. I'm talking about the size of your insula, a region of the brain deep in the cerebral cortex, which helps us feel and regulate our body. The insula can be enlarged through mindfulness practice. This is good news because the size and activity of the insula is directly correlated with quality of orgasm. As professor Marsha Lucas explains, "Having a bigger, juicier, busier insula can help you be better able to experience all of the fantastic bodily sensations and changes that are part of the real deal in sex."[4]

Sound good? So, what is mindful sex and how do you practice it? First, mindful sex frees you from the pressure to have "perfect" sex, look good, or do it "right." Mindful sex is an invitation into the mystery and beauty of your authentic sexuality. It will help you step outside of conditioned beliefs that might be dictating how you view and "do" sex, and breathe new vitality into your sexual experience.

For me, bringing mindfulness into my sexual experience was life changing. I became kinder, more compassionate with my body. I deepened my awareness of my own pleasure. And I began to feel safe enough to be honest with myself and my partner about what I was feeling and what I desired. Interestingly, being more connected to myself and sharing what I was feeling helped me feel more connected to my partner.

Practicing mindful sex softened and opened me. I experienced a new aliveness and vitality that spilled over into my daily life, accompanying me as I walked, danced, ate, sang, listened to music, or took a shower. I discovered greater tenderness, joy, and intimacy in all of my moments.

Mindful sex also emboldened me, giving me courage to trust my body, my desires, and my sexuality. It inspired a freedom, a playfulness, and an invitation to embrace all of my experience. No part left out. My fears, my desires, my vulnerabilities, my awkwardness, my orgasms, my silliness—everything was welcome.

Mindful sex continues to be a path of intimacy with myself and with life—a love affair that allows me to be a perpetual beginner, always learning, discovering, exploring, and growing. Every day I have the opportunity to bring greater tenderness, greater wonder, greater kindness to my sexuality.

Below are some ways to bring the three elements of mindfulness into your sexual experiences.

Intention: Reflect on your intentions, your hopes, and your desires around sex. Perhaps your hope is to foster greater intimacy in your relationship. Perhaps it is to experience greater pleasure and vitality. Perhaps it is to deepen your connection with your own body. Perhaps it is to create a baby. Whatever your intention, simply name it and allow it to guide you.

Attention: Bring your attention to the felt sensations of a sexual or sensual experience. Our body sensations anchor us in the present moment. Take some time to tune in to your own pleasure. As you focus your attention on your body, you will learn and understand what turns you on and enlivens you sexually. Become present with the sensations of touch, taste, smell, sight, and sound. If there are moments of discomfort, notice these, too. Welcome everything. Allow your attention to rest on the flow of changing sensations as they rise and pass. If you feel yourself getting distracted by criticism or judgments, gently bring your mind back to attending to your body. Perhaps enjoy a moment of breathing deeply and rest your attention on the sensations in your sexual centers. Close your eyes and allow yourself to be fully immersed in your experience here and now.

Attitude: Kindness and curiosity create an environment of openness that allows you to discover and explore. They create a container of safety for both you and your partner, where learning, play, intimacy, vulnerability, and exploration are fostered. Sex can make us feel incredibly tender, bringing out parts of ourselves that we often hide and protect. By enveloping ourselves and our partner in kindness, curiosity, and compassion, we allow our deepest vulnerabilities to be revealed. As my friend Jessica Graham, author of *Good Sex*, taught me: *vulnerability is hot.*[5]

Mindful Decision-Making

Another aspect of daily life deeply affected by mindfulness is decision-making. There's a pertinent story of a student who asks his wise teacher about how to make decisions:

> Student: "Teacher, how do I make good choices?"
> Teacher: "Experience."
> Student: "How do I gain experience?"
> Teacher: "Bad choices."

From this perspective, there are no mistakes; only experience. Each experience offers us an opportunity to learn and informs our next decision.

And yet this is not how we typically respond when something doesn't go the way we planned. We label it as "wrong" or a "mistake," followed by all sorts of negative self-talk and self-judgment.

What if instead we viewed our "mistake" as part of the process of learning, bringing us ever closer to our goals? This is the power of mindfulness, which teaches us how to trust that "even this is part of my evolution." By approaching each of our experiences as an opportunity for growth, we open ourselves to infinite possibilities for change and transformation.

This approach takes a bit of the pressure off when facing a decision—which, it turns out, is very important: Professor Barry Schwartz at Swarthmore College in Pennsylvania discovered that the biggest reason people fail to make a decision is their fear of making the wrong one.[6] He termed this the *paradox of choice*, empirically demonstrating that, paradoxically, the *more* choices we have, the *less* likely we are to make a choice—and if we do make a choice, the less likely we are to be satisfied with it.

This seems counterintuitive, but the data does not lie. For example, when asked if they'd prefer non-refundable or refundable plane tickets, just about everyone opts for refundable, desiring the greatest freedom of choice. However, in the study, those participants who were given refundable tickets were much less happy than those with nonrefundable tickets. The ones who had the freedom to choose from an infinite array of dates and times became anxious about choosing the *perfect* time to fly and ended up *less happy*.[7]

So, how do we make our best choices? First, we need to limit the number of options to those most relevant to what we truly want. This begins by getting clear on what your standards and goals are, and then to feel satisfied once you've reached them. Barry Schwartz refers to this as being a "satisficer" versus being a "maximizer." Research shows that satisficers—people who limit their options and don't keep endlessly looking for the perfect, best choice—are much happier and more successful.[8] Mindfulness helps us do this by keeping us in touch with our intentions and guiding us to zero in on what is most important and let go of distracting desires and impulses.

Another crucial step in making wise decisions is to pause and listen not just to our mental processes—the pros/cons list we keep running through our mind—but also to our emotions and to the cues our body gives us. As psychotherapist Esther Perel astutely notes, "The body often contains emotional truths that words can too easily gloss over."[9]

Renowned neuroscientist Antonio Damasio found that when the connection between the amygdala (the seat of our emotions) and the prefrontal cortex (the source of our higher-order reasoning) was cut as the result of injury, it led to an inability to make decisions.[10] The conclusion: in order to make wise decisions, we need to be able to draw on the wisdom of our body sensations/emotions coupled with our mental capacities.

Again, mindfulness comes to our aid. By attending to the sensations in our body as we explore the different options, we can connect with our emotions and route this information up to our cortex, where the highly developed frontal lobe is grappling with what to decide.

But we need to train this capacity to notice and listen to our body and our emotions. We can't just all of a sudden expect to tune in like this when hit with big decisions (e.g., "Should I marry this person?" "Should I take this job?"). We need to practice inner listening *every day* so that when the big decisions come, we are attuned and ready.

Mindfulness trains us in how to listen to our emotions and our bodies: *How does it feel in my body when I imagine making this decision? Do I feel calm and at ease? Is there a sense of relief? A sense of alignment?*

As we practice mindfulness in low-stakes situations (e.g. "Should I eat this for lunch?"), we deepen the feedback loop between body and brain. The more you practice, the stronger the feedback loop and the faster you can access it. What you practice grows stronger. So, when the stakes are high, you have developed a trustworthy pathway, aligning your emotional intuition with your cognitive intelligence.

In a recent study with undergraduates at Santa Clara University, we found that mindfulness training powerfully increased ethical decision-making.[11] The training focused on learning to attend to one's own values, thoughts, emotions, and body sensations instead of attempting to tell students what the "right" ethical choice should be. For example, instead of telling them "It's wrong to drink and drive," the process would be to explore with the students the values associated with safe driving, and how it feels in one's body to imagine drinking and causing harm.

Mindfulness helps decision-making become a process of personal inquiry as opposed to a purely top-down hierarchical and moralistic process of being told what is "right" versus what is "wrong."

Again, we can apply the three elements of mindfulness to decision-making:

Intention: Reflect on what your deepest hope is for the outcome of this decision. What do you value? How might you feel once you reach the "right" choice for you? Reflect on what choices and actions will lead to greater well-being for yourself and others.

Attention: Bring your full attention to your mental processes, your body sensations, and your emotional responses as you consider the decision. Listen deeply, welcoming all your emotions, sensations in the body, and thoughts as part of the listening process. Perhaps when you think about making a particular choice you feel a hollowness in your belly, or tightness in your throat. Perhaps as you reflect on a different choice you feel a sense of confidence and calm. Pay attention with your whole being; as Chuang Tzu said, "The hearing of the spirit is not limited to any one faculty, not to the ear or the mind."[12]

Attitude: Cultivate the attitudes of kindness and curiosity as you reflect on the decision you are trying to make. Welcome all of the concerns, ideas, emotions, and thoughts that arise. Allow yourself whatever reactions you are having to the different options. As the wise teacher Coquelicot Gilland once guided me, "Hold a quorum inside yourself, invite all of your voices. Listen deeply, with curiosity and kindness."[13] It is only through listening to all the voices that we can discover the truth and make wise decisions.

Mindfulness in the Workplace

Mindfulness is also valuable in the workplace, no matter what kind of work you do. Perhaps you've heard about corporations bringing mindfulness training into the workplace, and there's good reason why. Fortune 500 companies such as Google, Proctor & Gamble, Aetna, Facebook, and General Mills have been implementing large-scale mindfulness programs over the past few years. Thousands of employees have participated in these programs, and the data show a definite positive impact—from decreased stress, increased productivity and innovation, and enhanced decision-making to greater company loyalty and workplace satisfaction.

For example, Aetna, the nation's third-largest health insurer, collaborated with Duke University to study mindfulness training. The results: 28 percent of the participants reported decreased stress levels, 20 percent experienced improved sleep quality, 19 percent felt reduced pain—and productivity improved by 62 minutes per employee per week.[14]

One vice president at a Fortune 500 company shared this story of how practicing mindfulness affected his work life:

> I'm a driven person. I push people hard and get the best from them. At times I can push too hard, and I forget to pause and see the situation clearly. I'll never forget what happened when the lead project manager came to tell me she had misjudged the timeline, and her team was far behind schedule. Normally, I would have lost my temper, snapped at her, and demanded she get back on schedule. However, this time everything slowed down. I was able to take a breath and pause before responding. Instead of yelling, I asked her what the obstacles were and what she needed to

get back on track. We had a clear, focused conversation and came to a reasonable solution, albeit not my ideal. As she was leaving, she paused at the door, and said softly, "Thank you. I wasn't planning on sharing this, but my husband was recently diagnosed with cancer, and we have two young children at home, and I've been overwhelmed. Your understanding today meant a lot to me." I just stood there, the intensity of the emotions that welled up in me were surprising. I felt compassion for her challenges, and grateful that I'd been able to pause, instead of angrily reacting. I realized all of us are struggling, and there is always more to a story than there seems.

You can bring mindfulness into your work life by incorporating the three elements of mindfulness into your workday:

Intention: Reflect on your goals and aspirations for your work. What is most important? What do you value? Even if you realize that your work life is far different from what you value, you can set an intention to move in a direction that is more aligned. Write down your short- and long-term goals. Use this practice as a way to reset your compass, reconnecting with what is most important, and revisit those goals periodically to see if they still fit with your values, taking into consideration how you might begin to bridge the gap between where you are and where you want to be.

Attention: Commit to bringing your full attention to your work while you are at work. As we saw in chapter 4, multitasking has deleterious consequences both for our personal health and our effectiveness in the workplace. Commit to doing one task at a time with your complete attention. At the end of the workday, write down anything that was not completed so that you can mentally leave it at work and bring your full attention home with you. The key is to be present wherever you are.

Attitude: As we've learned, kindness and curiosity create an environment of psychological safety conducive to learning and collaboration. These attitudes also lead to greater innovation, creativity, and success. In fact, my colleagues and I recently published a study in *Harvard Business Review* demonstrating that a mindful attitude was associated with greater entrepreneurial skills, including creativity and innovation.[15]

Mindful Parenting

Like me, many of the people I work with have experienced both the triumphs and tribulations of being a parent. We love our children more than anything in the world, yet they can also be our greatest challenge. Here, too, mindful awareness can change things.

Mindful parenting does not mean being a "perfect parent." It means applying the skills we've been developing so we can be the best parents possible. It also means treating ourselves compassionately when we miss the mark. When we give ourselves another chance, we're more able to extend that same compassion to our children. Which is not to say that we give ourselves or our children a free pass to do whatever, whenever. Remember the wise Zen saying from chapter 2: "You're perfect as you are, and there is room for improvement." This is a wonderful message to model for our children, both in how we treat them and how we treat ourselves.

In this way, mindful parenting is an antidote to the guilt and shame so many of us carry about not being good enough. Mindfulness gives us perspective and helps us break the cycle of shame and knee-jerk reactivity that can escalate situations. When our child's behaviors trigger us, we are able to step back and see clearly instead of becoming emotionally hijacked. This doesn't mean that we won't get angry or upset; it means that we'll be aware of our emotions and learn to regulate them, putting us back in choice.

Mindful parenting will also help you become more attuned and responsive to your child's needs, thoughts, and feelings, helping to deepen and strengthen your relationship with your child. Our children want our presence more than anything else. It nourishes them in a way nothing else can. Mindfulness helps us attend to our children—it helps us *tend to* them.

Recent research shows that children who experience mindful parenting are less likely to use drugs, engage in risky behaviors, and have less depression and anxiety.[16] I delve into this research and more detailed methodology in the book *Mindful Discipline: A Loving Approach to Setting Limits and Raising an Emotionally Intelligent Child*, but you can get started right now just by applying the three elements of mindfulness:

Intention: Reflect on what is most important to you as a parent. To be more present with your child? To listen more? To play more? To connect more? To trust more? Write down your deepest aspirations. Keep them in the foreground by reflecting on them regularly. Let them motivate and guide you.

Attention: Practice bringing your full attention into the present moment with your child. I am struck by how often I catch myself doing other things while interacting with my son—cooking, checking email, packing up for work, et cetera. Perhaps it is similar for you? Remember: no blame. Life is busy. However, you can set aside a specific time each day when you will be completely with your child, doing nothing else. Protect this time from phone calls and all other interruptions. This will model and teach your child the value you place on sacred time to just be together, without distraction. In our complex and demanding world, our **most valuable asset** is no longer our time, it is our **attention**. Focusing our full attention on our children communicates to them that we value them.

> › *In our complex and demanding world, our **most valuable asset** is no longer our time, it is our **attention.***

Attitude: Infuse your interactions with your child with the attitudes of kindness and curiosity. "You made a new painting. Tell me about it, I'm interested." "You're listening to music. Could we listen together?" "You're really good at this video game. What do you like best about it?" "Oh! That's interesting." "Hm! What happened then?" "Wow. What was that like for you?" See if you can become truly interested, curious about your child's experience. Welcoming them in the loving embrace of your presence.

Mindful Eating

We all know that we need food to live, but our relationship with food is much more complex than simple survival. Food can be an ally, and it can also cause great harm. While obesity and eating disorders create enormous suffering, it's not just those with clinical diagnoses who experience challenges with eating. Most of us struggle with eating at one time or another. Some of us are yo-yo dieters. Some of us are genetically prone to issues with cholesterol. And some of us are so constantly on the go that we have trouble making time for nourishing meals.

On top of this, most of us are not present when we are eating. Think back over the last seven days. What were you doing while eating—driving, reading, talking, working, or watching TV? In fact, how many meals from the past week can you actually remember? Most of the time we eat on automatic pilot.

Mindfulness helps us counter our unconsciousness and reactivity around food. It involves bringing our full presence to the moment-to-moment experience of eating. As we eat mindfully, we are able to listen to the messages of our body, recognizing what foods our body wants as well as appreciating when we feel hungry and when we become full.

Mindfulness also helps us receive the joy and pleasure of eating, encouraging us to savor the touch, smell, texture, and taste of our food. Engaging all of our senses while we eat can transform the entire experience.

Intention: Before you begin eating, pause and reflect on your intention for eating: to nourish your body, to give it energy, to enjoy the food, to stay present.

Attention: As you begin to eat, bring your full attention to the moment. You can do this by heightening your senses: focus on what you are seeing, tasting, touching, and smelling. As we savor our food in this way, we are able to slow down, chewing each mouthful with care, which aids the digestive process. We can also pay attention to our level of hunger as we eat, and to the sensations in our body as it guides us in how much to eat.

Attitude: Bring a kind, curious attitude to eating. If you notice judgmental thoughts, see if you can bring kindness and curiosity to them. There is no right way to do this. Welcome all of your experience. Notice if this attitude of kindness and curiosity helps you become aware of something novel about the experience of eating or leads to any important insights.

PRACTICE   Mindful Eating

If you have done previous training in mindfulness, you may have come across this exercise. It's simply one of the best. You will need a raisin or some other small piece of fruit for this exercise. Sit in a comfortable position, relax your mind and body. Bring to mind your **intention** *(to stay present, curious, kind).*

Take a moment to reflect on the many elements, such as the rain, sunshine, earth, and air that have come together to create this food that will nourish you. Open to the feeling of gratitude for having food, and to all of the people who grew, picked, dried, packed, and transported this raisin so that you could hold it in your hands.

Now, bring your full **attention** to the raisin. Take note of its size, shape, color. If you're eating a raisin, perhaps reflect on how it used to be a grape and find where it was picked from the vine—the "belly button" of the raisin. As you're ready, hold the raisin or piece of fruit up to your nose, close your eyes, and receive its scent. Then, with eyes still closed, place it in your mouth, and without chewing, begin to move it around your mouth with your tongue. Notice all the sensations that begin to occur . . . increased saliva, the texture of the raisin, the dexterity of your tongue.

And as you are ready, bite into this small piece of fruit. Become aware of the explosion of flavor and the impact on your body. Bring your kind, curious *attitude* to all aspects of the experience. Chew slowly, noticing which teeth you use. Notice the movements of your magnificent tongue.

And then slowly, intentionally, swallow. Realize that this piece of fruit is now a part of you. Sit quietly and receive the experience.

In your journal, reflect on what you noticed, and how this experience was different from your typical way of eating. Perhaps make a commitment to eat one mindful meal this week, or perhaps just one mindful bite.

Slowing Down

One of the most important ways of bringing mindfulness into your daily life is by slowing down. This doesn't necessarily mean we have to go slow. It simply means that we move through life with less urgency, less pressure, less fear. This gives us more moments of choice where we can live aligned with our truest values.

Consider the famous Good Samaritan study from Princeton University.[17] Psychologists John Darley and Dan Batson gave an assignment to a group of seminary students studying to become ordained ministers: they were to prepare and then deliver a sermon on being a good Samaritan.

When the students arrived to give their sermon, half were told something like, "Oh no, you are late, you are supposed to give the sermon across campus. Hurry!" These students urgently ran off, worried they would miss their first sermon.

As they hurried across campus, they encountered a person who had been mugged and was in need of help (in reality, this was an actor pretending to have been mugged). Sadly—and ironically—the vast majority of these students ran past him in their haste to give their sermon about what it meant to be a good Samaritan!

Now, here's the flip side. When the other half of the students arrived at the university, they were gently told to head across campus to give their sermon. These students set out without the urgency and anxiety of their peers. When the same actor asked for help, a great many more of these students stopped and offered help.

The moral: when we feel rushed, overwhelmed, and pressured, it hinders our capacity to be intellectually and emotionally available. We miss important opportunities that surface in the present moment. By moving more slowly and mindfully, we are able to access all of our resources and engage with the full power available to us.

Mindful sex, mindful decision-making, mindfulness in the workplace, mindful parenting, and mindful eating are just a few of the truly infinite number of ways that mindfulness can become a part of everyday life. Whatever we do, wherever we do it, intention, attention, and attitude enrich our experience, liberate us to grow and change, and allow us to move through the world with greater ease. It's not magic, it's practice.

GOLD NUGGET   Pause and reflect on the highlights from this chapter and then choose one Gold Nugget you want to take with you and encode in your long-term memory. Write it down in your journal.

Sample Gold Nuggets:

- Mindfulness can be practiced in any moment.
- We can bring our intention, attention, and attitude into everything we do.
- We can turn the mundane into magic.

A MORE CONNECTED AND COMPASSIONATE WORLD

Being whole and simultaneously part
of a larger whole, we can change the world
simply by changing ourselves.

JON KABAT-ZINN

I settle into the middle seat of a United Airlines 737 and take some deep breaths as the plane thunders down the runway and the wheels leave the ground. I'm on my way to San Miguel de Allende, Mexico, to a conference exploring the intersection of science and culture. Normally I had looked forward to these conferences, but for the past month or two nothing could seem to lift my spirits. I'd been feeling disconnected and alone, filled with grief at the recent passing of my Grandpa Ben, who had been like a father to me.

As I was packing before I left, a friend told me that people in Mexico consider $2 bills to be auspicious. So, on my way to the airport, I'd stopped at the bank and tucked an envelope filled with $2 bills into my bag.

Arriving in San Miguel, I'm awed by the city's beauty. Color is everywhere. The cobblestone streets are lined with yellow and red two-toned buildings. White flowers spill from window boxes, twine around wrought-iron gates, and climb the hand-built walls of stone. People bustle about el Centro as a mariachi band plays, and the enticing smells of dulce de leche waft from corner cafes. Rising high above it all, the coral and magenta spires of the Parroquia de San Miguel Arcángel church look over the city like a proud parent watching over her child.

I notice a young mother sitting on the street, holding her baby girl in her arms, her young son standing next to her. I offer her my first $2 bill as I attempt to chat with her son, Diego. My Spanish is about equal to his three-year-old language skills, and his mother laughs as she listens. Her laughter is contagious, and we share in this most universal human language.

Feeling happier, I continue through the town, handing a $2 bill to a musician strumming her classic oblong cello, and another to a boy selling churros on the side of the road. But I still feel the whispers of loneliness looming in the back of my mind.

My week continues in much the same way. The conference is interesting; the food, music, and culture exquisite—but it seems that no matter what I do, I still feel alone, the quiet drumbeat of separation within.

Until my last morning in San Miguel.

I wake early, wanting to take one final stroll through the cobblestone streets. Near the end of my walk I see an old man with a walker. He is painstakingly making his way up the street, one imperceptible step at a time.

He is also clutching a large broom with bright red bristles. *He couldn't possibly be the street cleaner, could he?* Yet every couple of steps he pauses and braces himself with one hand on the walker, while with the other he sweeps the street with his red broom. I'm reminded of my Grandpa Ben: he had the same walker, the same perseverance, the same dignity.

I approach the man and smile. "Hola! You remind me of *mi abuelo*." He smiles back. I ask his name.

"Mario Morales," he replies, in a welcoming, self-possessed tone.

With an awkward gesture I offer him a $2 bill. Leaning the broom against his shoulder, he takes the bill and looks me in the eyes. I am struck by the intensity of our gaze. There is an aliveness there, belying his age and physical stature.

As our gaze deepens, I see Grandpa's eyes looking out at me. Loving me.

My eyes well up with tears. The abuelo continues to hold me with his loving eyes. Everything shifts. I am not the one giving to him—the "savior" helping the "one in need." My biases and blind spots are illuminated and I realize *I am the one receiving*. Beneath our differences, we belong to each other.

The Delusion of Separation

Mother Teresa observed decades ago: "The biggest disease today is not leprosy or tuberculosis but rather the feeling of not belonging." All too often we forget we are part of the web of life and instead insulate ourselves in a prison of separateness. Einstein refers to this prison as an "optical delusion of consciousness" that we have constructed through invisible psychological boundaries. These boundaries keep us feeling alone and isolated despite our hunger to feel connected and part of something larger than ourselves.

This epidemic of loneliness is leading to devastating consequences. Feeling isolated and alone is a greater risk factor for death and disease than either smoking or obesity. In fact, loneliness has become such a widespread issue that governments have now become involved: in 2018, the United Kingdom appointed Tracey Crouch as the first Minister for Loneliness.

To heal this epidemic of loneliness, we must free ourselves from the optical delusion of separateness.

Mindfulness helps us do this. It reminds us of our shared humanity and enables us to see ourselves and each other clearly. For example, research shows that even a brief mindfulness practice can reduce unconscious, or implicit, biases against people who seem different. In a study at Central Michigan University, students practiced mindfulness and were then given a standard test to measure their implicit bias.[1] Students who meditated for just 10 minutes showed less implicit bias toward race and age compared with a control group. This research highlights how mindfulness practice can help reduce preconceived judgments and biases, bringing greater awareness and clear seeing. As Ruth King beautifully puts it in her book *Mindful of Race*, "[Mindfulness] offers a way for us to slow down and to investigate our experiences with care and attention. It supports us in bearing witness to our racial distress and conditioning without distortion, elaboration, or judgment."[2]

Mindfulness can help us heal the illusory separation that comes from unexamined prejudice and bias. It helps us look directly at where racial perceptions live and can help shift our internal prejudices and subsequently our external racist structures.[3]

Mindfulness supports us in being vigilantly attuned to issues of privilege and power, biases and assumptions, while also recognizing that beneath it all, we belong to each other. This powerful reasoning helps us acknowledge and respect our differences, while at the same time recognizing our fundamental interconnection.

Together, this dialectic helps us recognize the harmful dichotomy of *us* versus *them*, remembering Maya Angelou's beautiful words: "We are more alike, my friends, than we are unalike."[4] Indeed, 99.9 percent of human DNA is identical.[5] The key then, is to recognize, learn about, and value differences, while simultaneously comprehending our profound interdependence.

The more we practice seeing our common humanity without glossing over our differences, the more we train and encourage our brain to bypass a conditioned and narrow mind-set. This shift can give rise to a natural compassion and a dedication to the greater good. This is not a top-down moralistic shift where we're helping others because it's the "right" thing to do. Instead, it's a bottom-up insight that arises from visceral understanding of a truth: everything is connected.

Imagine a simple example: if my left hand has a splinter, what does my right hand do? It removes the splinter, of course! We understand that the left hand and the right hand are parts of the same body. The same is true in life. As the Reverend Martin Luther King Jr. wrote in his letter from the Birmingham jail, "We are caught in an inescapable network of mutuality, tied in a single garment of destiny. Whatever affects one directly, affects all indirectly."[6] This and his other powerful quote from that letter, "Injustice anywhere is a threat to justice everywhere," highlight the interconnectedness of all human experience.

A More Connected and Compassionate World

The idea of our interconnectedness is not just some lofty spiritual ideal. Interdependence is a fundamental law of nature and is the predominant worldview of modern science, ecology, cybernetics, physics, culture, and systems theory. We live in a complex, interwoven system where everything affects everything else. Nothing is separate. As the renowned conservationist John Muir put it, "When we try to pick out anything by itself, we find it hitched to everything else in the universe."[7]

> *We live in a complex, interwoven system where everything affects everything else. Nothing is separate.*

So, how do we create a more connected and compassionate world? Einstein warns that we live in "a kind of prison . . . restricting us to our personal desires and to affection for a few persons nearest to us." He encourages us to "free ourselves from this prison by widening our circle of compassion."[8]

As we've learned, widening our circle of compassion begins with awareness — awareness of the biases and assumptions that separate us, awareness of power and privilege that oppress, and awareness of how compassion for others grows out of compassion for ourselves. Remember the veteran who had to practice forgiving himself before he could begin to heal his own pain and reach out to help others do the same? Or Samantha, who discovered how facing her breast cancer with self-compassion opened the path to connecting more fully with the community of pink ribbons surrounding and supporting her?

Mindfulness, self-compassion, and the practices that emerge from them help free us from the prison of isolation and the delusion of separation. These practices open our minds, awaken our hearts, and deepen our sense of connection with ourselves, each other, and our world. We begin to realize that we are never just practicing for ourselves. Transforming ourselves creates echoes in the universe. As we heal ourselves, we heal each other, and our world.

> We begin to realize that we are
> never just practicing for ourselves.
> Transforming ourselves creates echoes
> in the universe. As we heal ourselves,
> we heal each other, and our world.

PRACTICE **Interdependence**

Begin by settling the mind and body. Allow a soft smile to rest on your lips, not as a way to paper over how you are feeling, but simply to invite in rest and ease.

Bring your awareness to breathing. Just the simple sensations of breathing in and out. Feel how the breath is supporting you, oxygenating the body with each inhale, releasing stress and toxins with each exhale.

Begin to sense the beating of your heart. Become aware of how the heart is supporting you, sending blood carrying oxygen and nutrients to all the trillions of cells in your body.

Invite in a feeling of gratitude and kindness toward your breath, your heart, your body.

Begin to feel your body seated on the floor, and let your awareness expand to include the earth below you, supporting you. Allow yourself to rest into the earth, to feel held by the earth. Feel how there is nothing more you need to do in this moment.

Reflect on how the earth is supporting all beings equally, and that gravity is keeping all beings tethered to the earth. In fact, the renowned seventeenth-century scientist Sir Isaac Newton said that gravity is like God's love, treating each person equally.

Reflect on how this earth is connected to a solar system and a vast universe. And that all things—all humans, all animals, the earth, the sun, and the stars—are composed of the same matter, the same basic particles.

We are literally all made of stardust.

Feel the web of life into which we are born, from which we can never fall. Feel how you are part of this web. Nothing is separate.

Feel yourself resting in the heart of the universe.

And begin to send your good wishes to all beings, gently and silently repeating, "May all beings be peaceful. May all beings be safe and protected. May all beings be happy. May all beings be filled with love and kindness."

And then recognize that you are contained within the good wishes for all beings. Rest your attention once again on this one being sitting here. And silently direct the good wishes to yourself: "May I be peaceful. May I be safe and protected. May I be happy. May I be filled with love and kindness."

As you breathe in, you are breathing in this lovingkindness, and as you breathe out, you are sending this lovingkindness out. May all beings here and everywhere dwell with peace. May the earth dwell in peace.

And close by offering: May this practice be of benefit for all beings.

———————

GOLD NUGGET   Pause and reflect on the highlights from this chapter, and then choose one Gold Nugget you want to take with you and encode in your long-term memory. Write this down in your journal.

Sample Gold Nuggets:

- Mindfulness can help bring to awareness our unconscious biases, assumptions, power, and privilege.
- There is a powerful dialectic between honoring and celebrating our difference, while remembering that all things are interconnected.
- We belong to each other.
- Separateness is an optical delusion of consciousness.
- Transforming ourselves creates echoes in the universe.

you are not a drop in the ocean.
you are the entire ocean,
in a drop.   *RUMI*

11

"GOOD MORNING,
I LOVE YOU"

And did you get what you wanted
from this life, even so?
I did.
And what did you want?
To call myself beloved,
to feel myself beloved on the earth.

Late Fragment by **RAYMOND CARVER**
(written while dying of cancer)

Eleven years ago, I went through a painful divorce.

I was hurt and alone. The damage was irreparable and the choice to leave was inevitable, but I still felt like a failure. No one in my family had ever divorced. My grandparents had been married for seventy years; my parents forty. All my aunts and uncles had thriving marriages, my sister was (and still is) happily married to her college sweetheart, and my brother had just gotten engaged to the woman of his dreams. Marriage in my family was sacrosanct.

The prospect of upending my life was terrifying. But that was nothing compared to my fear of how the divorce would affect our three-year-old son, Jackson.

Despite my fears, I packed up everything I could fit into my tiny car, buckled Jackson into his car seat, and drove to Marin County, California, where my grandparents lived. I needed to be close to family. And Nana and Grandpa were my home.

Once we'd crossed the Golden Gate Bridge and exited at Sausalito, we passed a small apartment building with a "For Rent" sign out front. I could tell just from the outside that it was out of my price range, but they were holding an open house that day, so I figured I'd take a quick look around. The owner, a large man with striking features and ebony skin, answered the door.

He warmly greeted us: "I'm Ishmael—" and then, observing my face more closely, and my car out front with all my belongings visibly packed into it: "Looks like you're having a tough day."

I told him I'd just left my husband and was looking for a place to live. And then, much to my surprise, I burst into tears.

His reaction is one I will never forget. "Young lady, sounds like you need a break. How about if I reduce the rent?"

He had no reason to help me, but he did. We worked out the logistics and he introduced his nephew, who would be my landlord. As I left, he gently said, "Remember this when you can help someone else get back on their feet."

I never saw Ishmael again, but I will never forget his kindness.

A week later, a soft beam of sunshine woke me. I blinked my eyes open, taking in the bare walls surrounding me. I was lying on the floor of our new apartment with Jackson snuggled in my arms. We had no furniture, so I'd zipped together two sleeping bags to make a little nest for us. As the rising sun filled the room, I could feel my love for Jackson filling my heart. It gave me strength to keep going, one small step at a time.

Yet over the next several weeks, with each step forward, I seemed to take two backward. I was adjusting to life as a single parent, juggling childcare, and commuting three hours round-trip to teach at the university. My life felt overwhelming. This was not how I imagined things would be. I felt exhausted and hopeless.

I was trying so hard, but each morning I'd wake with the same aching pit of fear and shame in my gut—my monkey mind swinging between ruminations about the past: *If only I had . . .* and fears about the future: *How am I going to handle it when _____ happens?*

I couldn't seem to shake the self-judgment and the sense that I had failed. There was no space for self-compassion. No space for self-kindness. No space for joy.

Friends, family, and colleagues all saw the pain I was in. Many offered support and ideas.

One of my meditation teachers suggested I begin each day by saying, "I love you, Shauna." I immediately balked. *Yuck!* It felt so contrived, so inauthentic.

She noticed my hesitation and suggested, "How about simply saying, 'Good morning, Shauna'?" Then, with a wink, she added, "Try putting your hand on your heart when you say it. It will release oxytocin—which, as you know, is good for you."

She knew the science would win me over. The next morning, when I awoke, I resolutely put my hand on my heart, took a breath, and said, "Good morning, Shauna." Much to my surprise, it felt kind of nice. Instead of the avalanche of shame and anxiety that usually greeted me upon awakening, I felt a flash of kindness.

I practiced saying "Good morning, Shauna" every day, and over the next few weeks I began to notice subtle changes—a bit less harshness, a bit more kindness. Little did I know that this small practice would lead to big changes.

One Sunday morning, I was out for a walk in our new neighborhood and passed an old basketball gym. I was surprised to hear loud music and laughter pouring out onto the street. What could be making so much noise at 8:00 am on a Sunday?!

Curious, I peeked through the door and saw about two hundred people of all ages, shapes, sizes, and colors . . . dancing. Some were clearly professional dancers—others clearly were not. But all had one thing in common: a look of pure joy on their faces.

As a young girl, I had danced with the Pacific Ballet Conservatory and fallen in love with dance. I especially loved the performances, when somehow my mind quieted and the dance became a joyful expression of my soul.

But after my back surgery, I stopped dancing. My body was no longer a safe place. It was filled with pain. It didn't move the way I wanted it to—even a simple movement like glancing over my shoulder was awkward and disconnected. Dancing was out of the question.

Sixteen years post-surgery and just a few months after leaving my marriage, there I was, standing in the doorway watching all these people joyfully dancing. Seeing me peeking in like a hesitant schoolgirl, an older woman with shining silver hair motioned for me to join. I turned and fled.

The next Sunday I found myself walking by the same old gym. The music played like the Pied Piper and again I peered in, longing to dance but afraid to join. Over the next couple of weeks, my Sunday walks past the gym became as much a ritual as my "Good morning, Shauna" practice. But I didn't go in.

I longed to dance, to feel that freedom I remembered and loved so well, yet I didn't trust my body. I was terrified of trying to dance again—of feeling awkward and vulnerable in front of a bunch of strangers.

Then one Sunday, I set my intention to walk through that gym door and dance, no matter what. I committed to practicing an attitude of kindness and curiosity no matter what happened and no matter how I felt. That morning when I got to the gym, I went in.

I stood in a corner, alone, eyes closed, while the music and movement surged all around me. I tried to gently move my body, simply trying to feel it.

I didn't dance with anyone. I didn't even look at anyone. But slowly, my body began to move.

I continued to go every Sunday morning, and one millimeter at a time, I began to re-inhabit my body. I began to feel parts that had been completely numb. And as my body began to wake up, I became aware of the emotions that had gotten locked inside—loss, grief, vulnerability, rage.

As I danced, these emotions began to move through me. As I made space for them, they began to transform. Unexpectedly, a new emotion arose: compassion. I began to feel compassion for the young woman still inside, who had lived for so long in pain, feeling awkward and alone.

Then one day, the tears came.

First one, then two tears escaped my closed eyes, sliding down my cheeks. As I continued to dance, the river of tears released something, and my body began to spin—round and round, twirling, eyes closed. Whirling tears, snot, and sweat. No thoughts, no judgment.

And then a lightness filled my being, a freedom in my body: joy.

As the music began to fade, my movements slowed, and I gently lay down on the floor. I felt at peace. I felt hope.

"God circled this place on the map just for you," wrote the fourteenth-century Persian poet Hafiz.[1]

Maybe he was right. Maybe I was supposed to be here. My life wasn't how I expected, and it certainly was far from perfect. But that was okay. I could begin again.

One Sunday, I saw a man who danced as if his soul were choreographing every movement. I asked where he had learned to dance like that. He responded with one word: Esalen. When I got home I immediately Googled "Esalen" and learned it was the very same retreat center in Big Sur, California, where my father had taught when I was a young girl. And, in yet another coincidence, they were holding a dance workshop the following month—during the week of my birthday.

This would be my first birthday without my son, as he was going to be with his father at a long-scheduled family reunion in New York.

I decided to go!

Driving through the gates of Esalen, the first thing I saw was a magnificent garden with eight-foot sunflowers, rows of lettuces and dinosaur kale, and the lush fronds of a banana tree—a kaleidoscope of color. Even more extraordinary were the hot springs, on a rocky cliff overlooking the Pacific Ocean.

The next morning was my birthday. I woke just before dawn and headed straight for the hot springs. Cool mist from the ocean mingled with steam from the springs, blanketing the world around me. I eased into the steaming waters. The sky was starting to lighten, announcing dawn's arrival.

I put my hand on my heart, preparing to do my "Good morning, Shauna" practice. Something about the magic of the place, the enfolding arms of the water and the mist, evoked an image of my grandmother; and the next thing I knew, I was saying, "Good morning, I love you, Shauna. Happy birthday."

The dam around my heart gave way and a flood of love poured in. I felt my grandmother's love. I felt my mother's love. I felt my own self-love. A sense of peace flowed through my body like the one I'd experienced so many years ago at the waterfall temple in Thailand.

I wish I could tell you that my life has been a bubble of self-compassion ever since, and that I've never again experienced shame or self-judgment. But of course that's not true.

What is true is that I continue to practice. Every morning, I put my hand on my heart and say, "Good morning, I love you, Shauna." Some days I feel awkward, some days I feel lonely and raw, and some days I feel profound love. Whatever I feel, I keep practicing, and every morning, this pathway grows stronger.

The "Good Morning, I Love You" practice continued to evolve and expand over the years. I began greeting the sunshine, the birds chirping in my backyard, the flowering jasmine outside my bedroom window. One morning, I even sent a "Good morning, I love you" to the garbage truck that woke me up!

I began saying "Good morning, I love you" to Jackson even if he wasn't there, which eased the ache when he was away at his father's house. I began to say it to my dear friends and family, to people I was working with, to my students. Eventually I started sending this greeting out to the world. I even began sending a silent *good morning, I love you* to my ex-husband, whom I realized I'd been leaving out.

Eventually, I began to teach this practice to my students and my clients, and finally shared it in a TEDx talk. Now well over a million people have learned the "Good Morning, I Love You" practice.

I've been awed and inspired by the ripple effect of this practice, and how it has changed people's lives. Thousands of people have shared their own "Good Morning, I Love You" stories with me.

One five-year-old boy sent me a video of his practice. He sat, eyes closed, his little hand on his heart. He took a deep breath and bellowed, "Good morning, I love you, Nathan!" Then he peeked his eyes open and shyly whispered, "Good morning, I love YOU, too."

Another "Good Morning, I Love You" story began when

I received a note via Instagram from a young mother named Kristen. Her three-year-old son was in the hospital recovering from brain surgery. She wrote that she'd seen my TEDx talk and had been practicing with her son every day. I responded to her message and we realized she lived near Phoenix, where I would be teaching a workshop called *Messy Motherhood*. I invited her to attend.

As Kristen, four hundred other mothers, and I put our hands on our hearts and practiced "Good Morning, I Love You," the sense of connection and compassion was palpable. We expanded our "Good morning, I love you" to include all children facing illness, and to all of their parents. We continued to expand our circle of compassion in all directions, to all beings. Many of us were crying by the end of the practice. Tears of love, tears of hope. I received a letter from Kristen while I was writing this book. Her son, now four, is healthy and thriving; all brain scans are clear. She wrote, "(these practices) helped me get through one of the most difficult chapters of my life, and come out of it stronger and more connected to myself than I have ever been."

Another story came from Azar, a recently widowed seventy-year-old woman originally from Iran. We began working together to help with the loss of her husband. At that time, she was terrified of the world, having never navigated it alone. She also felt lonely and without love in her life. As she began to practice "Good Morning, I Love You," she began to slowly transform.

Azar began to engage in dance classes and poetry groups. A year later, she traveled alone for the first time in her life—to attend one of my mindfulness retreats. At the retreat, she shared with the group how this practice had changed her life, and how she says, "Good morning, I love you" to herself and to her late husband each day. She shared that it opened her up to feeling love and joy again.

Three years later, Azar was diagnosed with breast cancer. I

have never seen anyone fight harder for her life. She won. Azar now volunteers teaching mindfulness to support groups for women with cancer.

As I've witnessed how this simple practice has catalyzed change in so many lives, I've come to see it as a microcosm of all the other practices we've explored in this book. The "Good Morning, I Love You" practice aims our *intention* toward cultivating greater love for ourselves and others. It focuses our *attention* in the present moment. And it invites an *attitude* of kindness and curiosity toward whatever we experience.

"Good Morning, I Love You" is an intimate practice that spirals out into the world and back in again to our own heart. It is a simple yet powerful practice that has changed lives. I know it can change yours.

As we come to the last pages of our journey together, know that the seeds you have planted will continue to take root and blossom as you move through your life. Our collective efforts will continue to support and inspire each other. Every morning, as I say these words to myself, know that I am also sending them to you: "Good morning, I love you."

THE FULL PRACTICE
Good Morning, I Love You

I always do the "Good Morning, I Love You" practice first thing when I wake up. While lying in bed, I place my hand on my heart and take a moment to simply feel the connection; to receive this tender gesture of self-care.

Please continue with me:

- Place your hand on your heart. Focus on your palm. Feel your heart pulsing through your chest.

- Feel how your heart is taking care of you, sending oxygen and nutrients to the trillions of cells in your body. The heart knows exactly how to care for you—you don't have to control it or even think about it. Simply receive the nourishment.

- When you're ready, take a breath, and say, "Good morning, [your name]." or "Good morning, I love you, [your name]."

- Notice how this makes you feel. See if you can bring kindness and curiosity to however you are feeling. There is no right or wrong way to feel.

- Trust that you are planting the seeds of presence and compassion for yourself and that these seeds will grow and strengthen the neural substrates of self-love.

- Send these seeds of blessing out into the
  world, offering the phrase "Good Morning, I
  love you" to anyone who comes to mind.

- Recognize that we are never just practicing for
  ourselves. Everything we do has echoes in the universe.

If we create a habit of greeting ourselves with love each morning, these first moments of our day can transform the rest of the moments of our day, our lives, and the lives of others.

GOLD NUGGET   Pause and reflect on the highlights from this chapter and then choose one Gold Nugget you want to take with you and encode in your long-term memory. Write this down in your journal. Then review all the Gold Nuggets you have gathered through this journey together. These small gems are yours to support you and remind you of the wisdom that is always already here, within you. At some level you already know everything I have shared with you. This book is simply a reminder. May it be of benefit.

Dance, when you're broken open.
Dance, if you've torn the bandage off.
Dance in the middle of the fighting.
Dance in your blood.
Dance, when you are perfectly free.   *RUMI*

Acknowledgments

I bow in gratitude to the innumerable people whose voices are contained in the pages of this book.

I am grateful to the luminaries and teachers who have supported me on this path including Daniel Siegel, Jack Kornfield, Trudy Goodman Kornfield, Tara Brach, Rick Hanson, Jon Kabat-Zinn, Sylvia Boorstein, Sharon Salzberg, Shinzen Young, Roshi Joan Halifax, Gary Schwartz, Andrew Weil, James Baraz, Alfred Kaszniak, Roger Walsh, Frances Vaughan, Dean Ornish, Zindel Segal, Mark Williams, Arianna Huffington, Gabor Maté, Eileen Fisher, Shiva Rea, Lorin Roche, and Camille Maurine. Their courage and efforts to build bridges between East and West have paved the way for bringing mindfulness and compassion into mainstream culture.

I am also deeply grateful to the thousands of students, patients, and clients I have worked with. It has been a profound privilege to be invited into their lives; they have taught me, humbled me, and inspired me.

I also feel deeply blessed by the rich and diverse community of friends and colleagues that have supported me through this life, and in the writing of this book. I am grateful to my esteemed colleagues at Santa Clara University and inspired by their dedication to social justice, cultural diversity, and issues of power and privilege. I am also grateful to Kristin Neff, Ann Curtis, Juna Mustad, Lucy Caldwell, Ingrid Sanders, Ann and Dean Ornish, Robyn Thomas, David Emanuel, Maya Katherine, Sarah Trost, Sarah Eden Davis, Robin Bitner, Jessica Graham, Cassi Vieten, Elissa Eppel, Diane Jonte-Pace, Diane Dreher, Richard Joannides, Hans Keeling, Arie Fabian, Martin Sachs, Daria Gershman,

Keith Sedwick, Tristan and Jennifer Simon, Miranda McPherson, Dana Kline, Peter and Allisson Bauman, Michael Hebb, Amishi Jha, Dacher Keltner, Victoria Maizes, Teja Bell, Anne Cushman, Christine Carter, Jessie Martinez, Mateo, Sophie Van Garnier, Lauren Bitner, Miriam Burke, Victoria Maizes, Lisa Rueff, Tim Chang, Mike Ameci, Corey Maas, Wendy Snyder, Coqulicot Gilland, Mark Coleman, Lori Schwanbeck, Azar and Gloria, Pete and Ali Yiangou, Loren Shuster, Donna Carol, Donna Simmons, Susan Bauer-Wu, J. Wallace Nichols, Shien-Lin Sun, Nicole Patrice, Lisa Rueff, Cornelia Holden, Mark and Lisa Levine, Ellen Cutler, Theresa Black, Heather and Jake Rosenstein, Scott Rogers, Jaqueline Chan, Cy and Susan Britto, Sergio Lialin, James Scott, Amy Ricafrente, Brad Balukjian. Rebecca Tate, Mathew Shafe, Bokura Kimiko, John Astin, Michael Solomon, Andreas Kuefer, Brent and Alex Bolthouse, the Connan family, the Witt family, Karla and Lydel Toye, and Luke, Caroline, and Lawson Tichy.

I am also profoundly grateful to my fairy godmother Emilie Murphy and the entire Nimocks-Murphy family. And to Cathy, David, Aaron and Lauren Krinsky, who have been lifelong family.

This book would not exist if not for the insightful and ardent editorial skills of Toni Poynter, the inspiration and humor of Shanan Sabin, the dedication to details of Selma Moeller, and the utter brilliance and generosity of Joseph Romm. I am also grateful to Tami Simon, founder of Sounds True and Caroline Pincus, senior editor, who have dedicated themselves to bringing ideas to life that will make the world a better place. I am grateful to my talented literary agent Celeste Fine who believed in this book from the first moment, and to Kristine Carlson, whose faith and loving guidance throughout have been invaluable.

I offer a deep bow of acknowledgment to Spirit Rock Meditation Center, where I have sat over forty meditation retreats, and experienced deep healing and profound love. I am also grateful to the Esalen Institute, and especially to Cheryl Fraenzl for over a decade of support, encouragement, and faith in my teaching. Portions of this manuscript were written on Esalen's sacred land, and its magic is woven into the fabric of this book.

I am grateful beyond words to my family. To my parents Deane and Johanna, who first introduced me to mindfulness and who have always supported me in finding my piece in the cosmic puzzle. To my grandparents, Ben and Nancy Freedman, whose wise and compassionate souls live inside of me. To my beloved son Jackson, for teaching me the meaning of unconditional love. To my dear sisters, Jena and Desi, brothers, Josh and Bret, and my extraordinary aunties, uncles, cousins, nephews and niece. And to William Tichy, thank you for opening my heart and always holding my hand.

Finally, I am grateful to you, dear reader. Thank you for your willingness and courage to go on this journey with me. At some level, you already know the essence of everything I have shared with you. This book is simply a reminder. May it be of benefit.

Notes

Chapter 1: A Monk's Whisper

1. Jon Kabat-Zinn, *Wherever You Go, There You Are: Mindfulness Meditation in Everyday Life* (New York: Hyperion, 1994).
2. Shauna L. Shapiro and Gary E. Schwartz, "The Role of Intention in Self-Regulation: Toward Intentional Systemic Mindfulness," in *Handbook of Self-Regulation*, ed. Monique Boekaerts, Paul R. Pintrich, and Moshe Zeidner (New York: Academic Press, 1999), 253–73, doi. org/10.1016/B978-012109890-2/50037-8.
3. Philip Brickman, Dan Coates, and Ronnie Janoff-Bulman, "Lottery Winners and Accident Victims: Is Happiness Relative?" *Journal of Personality and Social Psychology* 36, no. 8 (August 1978), 917–27, dx.doi.org/10.1037/0022-3514.36.8.917.
4. Daniel Goleman and Richard J. Davidson, *Altered Traits: Science Reveals How Meditation Changes Your Mind, Brain, and Body* (New York: Avery, 2018).

Chapter 2: The Miracle of Neuroplasticity

1. Tara Brach, *Radical Acceptance: Embracing Your Life with the Heart of a Buddha* (New York: Bantam Books, 2004).
2. Eleanor A. Maguire et al., "Navigation-Related Structural Change in the Hippocampi of Taxi Drivers," *Proceedings of the National Academy of Sciences* 97, no. 8 (April 11, 2000): 4398–403, doi.org/10.1073/pnas.070039597.
3. Sara W. Lazar et al., "Meditation Experience Is Associated with Increased Cortical Thickness," *Neuroreport* 16, no. 17 (November 28, 2005): 1893–97, doi.org/10.1097/01.wnr.0000186598.66243.19.
4. Alvaro Pascual-Leone et al., "Modulation of Muscle Responses Evoked by Transcranial Magnetic Stimulation during the Acquisition of New Fine Motor Skills," *Journal of Neurophysiology* 74, no. 3 (September 1995): 1037–45, doi.org/10.1152 /jn.1995.74.3.1037.
5. Angela Duckworth, *Grit: Why Passion and Resilience Are the Secrets to Success* (London: Vermilion, 2017).
6. Daniel J. Siegel, *The Developing Mind, Second Edition: How Relationships and the Brain Interact to Shape Who We Are* (New York: Guilford Press, 2012), 19.

7.   Peter M. Gollwitzer and Paschal Sheeran, "Implementation Intentions and Goal Achievement: A Meta-Analysis of Effects and Processes," *Advances in Experimental Social Psychology* 38 (2006): 69–119, doi. org/10.1016/S0065-2601(06)38002-1.

8.   Jack Kornfield, "What Really Heals and Awakens: Highlights from Symposium 2018," *Psychotherapy Networker*, May/June 2018, psychotherapynetworker.org/magazine/article/1163 /what-really-heals-and-awakens.

9.   Rick Hanson and Forrest Hanson, *Resilient: How to Grow an Unshakable Core of Calm, Strength, and Happiness* (New York: Harmony Books, 2018).

Chapter 3: Mindfulness: Seeing Clearly

1.   Shauna L. Shapiro et al., "Contemplation in the Classroom: A New Direction for Improving Childhood Education," *Educational Psychology Review* 27, no. 1 (March 2015): 1–30, doi.org/10.1007 /s10648-014-9265-3.

2.   Jon Kabat-Zinn et al., "Influence of a Mindfulness Meditation -Based Stress Reduction Intervention on Rates of Skin Clearing in Patients with Moderate to Severe Psoriasis Undergoing Phototherapy (UVB) and Photochemotherapy (PUVA)," *Psychosomatic Medicine* 60, no. 5 (September 1998): 625–32, doi.org/10.1097/00006842-199809000-00020.

3   Shauna L. Shapiro, Gary E. Schwartz, and Ginny Bonner, "Effects of Mindfulness-Based Stress Reduction on Medical and Premedical Students," *Journal of Behavioral Medicine* 21, no. 6 (December 1998): 581–99, doi.org/10.1023/A:1018700829825.

4.   Matthieu Ricard, Antoine Lutz, and Richard J. Davidson, "Neuroscience Reveals the Secrets of Meditation's Benefits," *Scientific American*, November 2014, 38–45, scientificamerican.com/article /neuroscience-reveals-the-secrets-of-meditation-s-benefits/; Yuna L. Ferguson and Kennon M. Sheldon, "Trying to Be Happier Really Can Work: Two Experimental Studies," *The Journal of Positive Psychology* 8, no. 1 (January 2013): 23–33, doi.org/10.1080 /17439760.2012.747000.

5.   Aubrey M. Toole and Linda W. Craighead, "Brief Self-Compassion Meditation Training for Body Image Distress in Young Adult Women," *Body Image* 19 (December 2016): 104–12, doi.org/10.1016/j. bodyim.2016.09.001; Antoine Lutz et al., "Regulation of the Neural Circuitry of Emotion by Compassion Meditation: Effects of Meditative Expertise," *PLOS ONE* 3, no. 3 (March 2008): E1897, doi. org/10.1371/journal.pone.0001897.

6. Daniel A. Monti et al., "A Randomized, Controlled Trial of
    Mindfulness-Based Art Therapy (MBAT) for Women with Cancer,"
    Psycho-Oncology 15, no. 5 (May 2006): 363–73,
    doi.org/10.1002/pon.988; Virginia P. Henderson et al., "A
    Randomized Controlled Trial of Mindfulness-Based Stress Reduction
    for Women With Early-Stage Breast Cancer Receiving Radiotherapy,"
    Integrative Cancer Therapies 12, no. 5 (January 2013): 404–13, doi.
    org/10.1177/1534735412473640; Maja Johannsen et al., "Efficacy
    of Mindfulness-Based Cognitive Therapy on Late Post-Treatment
    Pain in Women Treated for Primary Breast Cancer: A Randomized
    Controlled Trial," *Journal of Clinical Oncology* 34, no. 28 (October
    2016): 3390–99, doi.org/10.1200
    /JCO.2015.65.0770.

7. Anna Kozlowski, "Mindful Mating: Exploring the Connection
    Between Mindfulness and Relationship Satisfaction," *Sexual and
    Relationship Therapy* 28, no. 1–2 (2013): 92–104, doi.org/10.1080
    /14681994.2012.748889.

8. Robert W. Roeser et al., "Mindfulness Training and Reductions in
    Teacher Stress and Burnout: Results from Two Randomized, Waitlist-
    Control Field Trials," *Journal of Educational Psychology* 105, no. 3
    (August 2013): 787–804, doi.org/10.1037/a0032093.

9. Eric L. Garland et al., "Testing the Mindfulness-to-Meaning Theory:
    Evidence for Mindful Positive Emotion Regulation from a Reanalysis
    of Longitudinal Data," *PLOS ONE* 12, no. 12 (December 2017):
    E0187727, doi.org/10.1371/journal
    .pone.0187727.

10. Roeser et al., "Mindfulness Training," 787–804; Shauna L. Shapiro,
    David E. Shapiro, and Gary E. R. Schwartz, "Stress Management in
    Medical Education: A Review of the Literature," *Academic Medicine*
    75, no. 7 (July 2000): 748–59.

11. Lone O. Fjorback et al., "Mindfulness-Based Stress Reduction and
    Mindfulness-Based Cognitive Therapy: A Systematic Review of
    Randomized Controlled Trials," *Acta Psychiatrica Scandinavica* 124,
    no. 2 (August 2011): 102–19, doi.org/10.1111
    /j.1600-0447.2011.01704.x; Monti et al., "A Randomized, Controlled
    Trial of Mindfulness-Based Art Therapy," 363–73.

12. John J. Miller, Ken Fletcher, and Jon Kabat-Zinn, "Three-Year
    Follow-Up and Clinical Implications of a Mindfulness Meditation-
    Based Stress Reduction Intervention in the Treatment of Anxiety
    Disorders." *General Hospital Psychiatry* 17, no. 3 (May 1995):
    192–200, doi.org/10.1016/0163-8343(95)00025-M.

13. Yi-Yuan Tang et al., "Short-Term Meditation Training Improves
    Attention and Self-Regulation," *Proceedings of the National Academy of*

Sciences 104, no. 43 (November 2007), 17152–56, doi.org/10.1073/pnas.0707678104.

14. Britta K. Hölzel et al., "Mindfulness Practice Leads to Increases in Regional Brain Gray Matter Density," *Psychiatry Research-Neuroimaging* 191, no. 1 (January 2011): 36–43, doi.org/10.1016/j.pscychresns.2010.08.006.

15. Izabela Lebuda, Darya L. Zabelina, and Maciej Karwowski. "Mind Full of Ideas: A Meta-Analysis of the Mindfulness-Creativity Link," *Personality And Individual Differences* 93 (April 2016): 22–26, doi.org/10.1016/j.paid.2015.09.040.

16. Lebuda, Zabelina, and Karwowski, "Mind Full of Ideas," 22–26.

17. Michael D. Mrazek et al., "Mindfulness Training Improves Working Memory Capacity and GRE Performance While Reducing Mind Wandering," *Psychological Science* 24, no. 5 (May 2013): 776–81, doi.org/10.1177/0956797612459659; Yu-Qin Deng, Song Li, and Yi-Yuan Tang, "The Relationship Between Wandering Mind, Depression and Mindfulness," *Mindfulness* 5, no. 2 (April 2014): 124–28, doi.org/10.1007/s12671-012-0157-7; Matthew A. Killingsworth and Daniel T. Gilbert, "A Wandering Mind Is an Unhappy Mind," *Science*, November 12, 2010, science.sciencemag.org/content/330/6006/932/tab-figures-data.

18. Brian D. Ostafin and Kyle T. Kassman, "Stepping Out of History: Mindfulness Improves Insight Problem Solving," *Consciousness and Cognition* 21, no. 2 (June 2012): 1031–36, doi.org/10.1016/j.concog.2012.02.014.

19. Stephanie L. Bowlin and Ruth A. Baer, "Relationships Between Mindfulness, Self-Control, and Psychological Functioning," *Personality and Individual Differences* 52, no. 3 (February 2012): 411–15, doi.org/10.1016/j.paid.2011.10.050.

20. Richard J. Davidson et al., "Alterations in Brain and Immune Function Produced by Mindfulness Meditation," *Psychosomatic Medicine* 65, no. 4 (July–August 2003): 564–70, doi.org/10.1097/01.PSY.0000077505.67574.E3.

21. Asfandyar Khan Niazi and Shaharyar Khan Niazi, "Mindfulness-Based Stress Reduction: A Non-Pharmacological Approach for Chronic Illnesses," *North American Journal of Medical Sciences* 3, no. 1 (January 2011): 20–23, doi.org/10.4297/najms.2011.320.

22. Jon Kabat-Zinn, "An Outpatient Program in Behavioral Medicine for Chronic Pain Patients Based on the Practice of Mindfulness Meditation: Theoretical Considerations and Preliminary Results," *General Hospital Psychiatry* 4, no. 1 (April 1982): 33–47, doi.org/10.1016/0163-8343(82)90026-3.

23. Perla Kaliman et al., "Rapid Changes in Histone Deacetylases and Inflammatory Gene Expression in Expert Meditators," *Psychoneuroendocrinology* 40 (February 2014): 96–107, doi.org/10.1016/j.psyneuen.2013.11.004.

24. Niazi and Niazi, "Mindfulness-Based Stress Reduction," 20–23.

25. Rose H. Matousek, Patricia L Dobkin, and Jens Pruessner. "Cortisol as a Marker for Improvement in Mindfulness-Based Stress Reduction," *Complementary Therapies in Clinical Practice* 16, no. 1 (February 2010): 13–19, doi.org/10.1016/j.ctcp.2009.06.004.

26. Shauna L. Shapiro et al., "The Efficacy of Mindfulness-Based Stress Reduction in the Treatment of Sleep Disturbance in Women with Breast Cancer: An Exploratory Study," *Journal of Psychosomatic Research* 54, no. 1 (January 2003): 85–91, doi.org/10.1016 /S0022-3999(02)00546-9; Jason C. Ong, Shauna L. Shapiro, and Rachel Manber, "Combining Mindfulness Meditation with Cognitive-Behavior Therapy for Insomnia: A Treatment-Development Study." *Behavior Therapy* 39, no. 2 (June 2008): 171–82, doi. org/10.1016/j.beth.2007.07.002; Jason C. Ong et al., "A Randomized Controlled Trial of Mindfulness Meditation for Chronic Insomnia," *Sleep* 37, no. 9 (September 2014): 1553–63, doi.org/10.5665/ sleep.4010.

27. Hölzel et al., "Mindfulness Practice," 36–43; Lazar et al., "Meditation Experience," 1893–97.

28. Tonya L. Jacobs et al., "Intensive Meditation Training, Immune Cell Telomerase Activity, and Psychological Mediators," *Psychoneuroendocrinology* 36, no. 5 (June 2011): 664–81, doi.org/10.1016/j.psyneuen.2010.09.010.

29. Daniel J. Siegel, "Mindful Awareness, Mindsight, and Neural Integration," *The Humanistic Psychologist* 37, no. 2 (April–June 2009): 137–58, doi.org/10.1080/08873260902892220; Daniel J. Siegel, "Mindfulness Training and Neural Integration: Differentiation of Distinct Streams of Awareness and the Cultivation of Well-Being," *Social Cognitive and Affective Neuroscience* 2, no. 4 (December 2007): 259–63, doi.org/10.1093 /scan/nsm034.

30. Amishi Jha, associate professor of psychology, University of Miami, in discussion with the author, March 2019.

Chapter 4: The Three Pillars of Mindfulness: Intention, Attention, Attitude

1. Yuna L. Ferguson and Kennon M. Sheldon, "Trying to Be Happier

Really Can Work: Two Experimental Studies," *The Journal of Positive Psychology* 8, no. 1 (January 2013): 23–33, doi.org/10.1080/17439760.2012.747000.

2. Roger Bohn and James Short, "Measuring Consumer Information," *International Journal of Communication* 6 (2012): 980–1000, ijoc.org/index.php/ijoc/article/viewFile/1566/743.

3. Herbert A. Simon, "Designing Organizations for an Information-Rich World," in *Computers, Communication, and the Public Interest*, ed. Martin Greenberger (Baltimore, MD: Johns Hopkins Press, 1971), 40–41.

4. American Psychological Association, "Multitasking: Switching Costs," March 20, 2006, apa.org/research/action/multitask.

5. Robert D. Rogers and Stephen Monsell, "The Costs of a Predictable Switch Between Simple Cognitive Tasks," *Journal of Experimental Psychology: General* 124, no. 2 (June 1995): 207–31, doi.org/10.1037/0096-3445.124.2.207; Melina R. Uncapher and Anthony D. Wagner, "Minds and Brains of Media Multitaskers: Current Findings and Future Directions," *Proceedings of the National Academy of Sciences* 115, no. 40 (October 2018): 9889–96, doi.org/10.1073/pnas.1611612115.

6. Gloria Mark, Daniela Gudith, and Ulrich Klocke, "The Cost of Interrupted Work: More Speed and Stress," *Proceedings of the SIGCHI Conference on Human Factors in Computing Systems* 2008, 107–10, ics.uci.edu/~gmark/chi08-mark.pdf.

7. Christopher K. Germer, Ronald D. Siegel, and Paul R. Fulton, eds., *Mindfulness and Psychotherapy* (New York: Guilford Press, 2005).

8. Matthew A. Killingsworth and Daniel T. Gilbert, "A Wandering Mind Is an Unhappy Mind," *Science*, November 12, 2010, science.sciencemag.org/content/330/6006/932/tab-figures-data.

9. Paul Tillich, *Love, Power, and Justice: Ontological Analyses and Ethical Applications* (New York: Oxford University Press, 1960).

10. Davide Rigoni, Jelle Demanet, and Giuseppe Sartoni, "Happiness in Action: The Impact of Positive Effect on the Time of the Conscious Intent to Act," *Frontiers in Psychology* (2015), doi.org/10.3389/fpsyg.2015.01307.

11. Matthias J. Gruber, Bernard D. Gelman, and Charan Ranganath, "States of Curiosity Modulate Hippocampus-Dependent Learning via the Dopaminergic Circuit," *Neuron* 84, no. 2 (October 2014): 486–96, doi.org/10.1016/j.neuron.2014.08.060; Min Jeong Kang et al., "The Wick in the Candle of Learning: Epistemic Curiosity Activates Reward Circuitry and Enhances Memory," *Psychological Science* 20, no. 8 (August 2009), 963–73,

doi.org/10.1111/j.1467-9280.2009.02402.x; Judson Brewer, "Mindfulness Training for Addictions: Has Neuroscience Revealed a Brain Hack by which Awareness Subverts the Addictive Process?" *Current Opinion in Psychology* 28 (August 2019): 198–203, doi.org/10.1016/j.copsyc.2019.01.014.

12. Beth Rieken et al., "Exploring the Relationship between Mindfulness and Innovation in Engineering Students" (paper presented at the American Society for Engineering Education Annual Conference, Columbus, OH, June 25–28, 2017).

13. Todd B. Kashdan et al., "The Five-Dimensional Curiosity Scale: Capturing the Bandwidth of Curiosity and Identifying Four Unique Subgroups of Curious People," *Journal of Research in Personality* 73 (April 2018): 130–49, doi.org/10.1016/j.jrp.2017.11.011.

Chapter 5: Self-Compassion: Your Inner Ally

1. Christopher K. Germer and Kristin D. Neff, "Self-Compassion in Clinical Practice," *Journal of Clinical Psychology* 69, no. 8 (August 2013): 856–67, doi.org/10.1002/jclp.22021.

2. Jules Feiffer, "I Grew Up to Have My Father's Looks," 1976, pen and ink on paper, 7.5 x 13.7" (19 x 34.8 cm), via Artnet, accessed December 02, 2018, artnet.com/artists/jules-feiffer/i-grew-up-to -have-my-fathers-looks-osXdy07J8D04CdF44Fzx_A2.

3. Claire E. Adams and Mark R. Leary, "Promoting Self-Compassionate Attitudes Toward Eating Among Restrictive and Guilty Eaters," *Journal of Social and Clinical Psychology* 26, no. 10 (October 2007): 1120–44, doi.org/10.1521/jscp.2007.26.10.1120.

4. Sidney J. Blatt, Joseph P. D'Affitti, and Donald M. Quinlan, "Experiences of Depression in Normal Young Adults," *Journal of Abnormal Psychology* 85, no. 4 (August 1976): 383–89, doi.org/10.1037/0021-843X.85.4.383; Golan Shahar et al., "Self-Criticism and Depressive Symptomatology Interact to Predict Middle School Academic Achievement," *Journal of Clinical Psychology* 62, no. 1 (January 2006): 147–55, doi.org/10.1002 /jclp.20210; Rui C. Campos, Avi Besser, and Sidney J. Blatt, "Recollections of Parental Rejection, Self-Criticism and Depression in Suicidality," *Archives of Suicide Research* 17, no. 1 (February 2013): 58–74, doi.org/10.1080/13811118.2013.748416.

5. Brené Brown, *I Thought It Was Just Me (But It Isn't): Women Reclaiming Power and Courage in a Culture of Shame* (New York: Gotham, 2007).

6. Paul Gilbert and Chris Irons, "Focused Therapies and Compassionate

Mind Training for Shame and Self-Attacking," in *Compassion: Conceptualisations, Research and Use in Psychotherapy*, ed. Paul Gilbert (London: Routledge, 2005), 263–325.

7.   Juliana G. Breines and Serena Chen, "Self-Compassion Increases Self-Improvement Motivation," *Personality and Social Psychology Bulletin* 38, no. 9 (2012): 1133–43, doi.org/10.1177/0146167212445599.

8.   Kristin Neff, associate professor, University of Texas at Austin, in discussion with the author, 2017.

9.   Kristin Neff and Christopher Germer, *The Mindful Self-Compassion Workbook: A Proven Way to Accept Yourself, Build Inner Strength, and Thrive* (New York: Guilford Press, 2018).

Chapter 6: The Five Roadblocks to Self-Compassion: How to Overcome Them

1.   Kristin Neff and Christopher Germer, *The Mindful Self-Compassion Workbook: A Proven Way to Accept Yourself, Build Inner Strength, and Thrive* (New York: Guilford Press, 2018).

2.   Helen Rockliff et al., "A Pilot Exploration of Heart Rate Variability and Salivary Cortisol Responses to Compassion-Focused Imagery," *Clinical Neuropsychiatry: Journal of Treatment Evaluation* 5, no. 3 (2008): 132–39.

3.   Kristin D. Neff and S. Natasha Beretvas. "The Role of Self-Compassion in Romantic Relationships," *Self and Identity* 12, no. 1 (2013): 78–98, doi.org/10.1080/15298868.2011.639548.

4.   Jia Wei Zhang and Serena Chen, "Self-Compassion Promotes Personal Improvement From Regret Experiences via Acceptance," *Personality and Social Psychology Bulletin* 42, no. 2 (2016): 244–58, doi.org/10.1177/0146167215623271; Juliana G. Breines and Serena Chen, "Self-Compassion Increases Self-Improvement Motivation," *Personality and Social Psychology Bulletin* 38, no. 9 (2012): 1133–43, doi.org/10.1177/0146167212445599.

5.   Regina Hiraoka et al., "Self-Compassion as a Prospective Predictor of PTSD Symptom Severity Among Trauma-Exposed U.S. Iraq and Afghanistan War Veterans," *Journal of Traumatic Stress* 28, no. 2 (April 2015): 127–33, doi.org/10.1002/jts.21995; Katherine A. Dahm et al., "Mindfulness, Self-Compassion, Posttraumatic Stress Disorder Symptoms, and Functional Disability in U.S. Iraq and Afghanistan War Veterans," *Journal of Traumatic Stress* 28, no.5 (October 2015): 460–64, doi.org/10.1002/jts.22045.

6.   David A. Sbarra, Hillary L. Smith, and Matthias R. Mehl, "When Leaving Your Ex, Love Yourself: Observational Ratings of

Self-Compassion Predict the Course of Emotional Recovery Following Mar*ital Separation," Psychological Science* 23, no. 3 (March 2012): 261–69, doi.org/10.1177/0956797611429466.

7. Neff and Germer, *The Mindful Self-Compassion Workbook.*

Chapter 7: Six Practices for Tough Times

1. Cited in Jack Kornfield, *A Lamp in the Darkness* (Boulder, CO: Sounds True, 2014), 56.
2. Shinzen Young, *Natural Pain Relief: How to Soothe and Dissolve Physical Pain with Mindfulness* (Boulder, CO: Sounds True, 2011).
3. Frank Ostaseski, *The Five Invitations: Discovering What Death Can Teach Us about Living Fully* (New York: Flatiron Books, 2019).
4. Daniel Goleman, *Emotional Intelligence: Why It Can Matter More than IQ* (London: Bloomsbury, 1996).
5. James J. Gross, "Emotion Regulation: Affective, Cognitive, and Social Consequences," *Psychophysiology* 39, no. 3 (May 2002): 281–91, doi. org/10.1017/S0048577201393198.
6. Kevin N. Ochsner et al., "Rethinking Feelings: An fMRI Study of the Cognitive Regulation of Emotion," *Journal of Cognitive Neuroscience* 14, no. 8 (November 2002): 1215–29, doi.org/10.1162/089892902760807212.
7. J. David Creswell et al., "Neural Correlates of Dispositional Mindfulness During Affect Labeling," *Psychosomatic Medicine* 69, no. 6 (July–August 2007): 560–65, doi.org/10.1097/PSY.0b013e3180f6171f.
8. Arthur J. Deikman, *The Observing Self: Mysticism and Psychotherapy* (Boston: Beacon Press, 1982).
9. Jon Kabat-Zinn, *Full Catastrophe Living: Using the Wisdom of Your Body and Mind to Face Stress, Pain, and Illness* (New York: Delacorte Press, 1990), 297.
10. Shauna L. Shapiro et al., "Mechanisms of Mindfulness," *Journal of Clinical Psychology* 62, no. 3 (March 2006): 373–86, doi.org/10.1002/jclp.20237.
11. Giacomo Rizzolatti et al., "Premotor Cortex and the Recognition of Motor Actions," *Cognitive Brain Research* 3, no. 2 (April 1996): 131–41, doi.org/10.1016/0926-6410(95)00038-0.
12. Boris C. Bernhardt and Tania Singer, "The Neural Basis of Empathy," *Annual Review of Neuroscience* 35, no. 1 (July 2012): 1–23, doi.org/10.1146/annurev-neuro-062111-150536
13. Daniel Goleman and Richard J. Davidson, *Altered Traits: Science Reveals How Meditation Changes Your Mind, Brain, and Body* (New York: Avery, 2018).

14. Elisha Goldstein, "Our Barriers to Love: Monday's Mindful Quote from Rumi," PsychCentral.com, last updated February 15, 2010, blogs. psychcentral.com/mindfulness/2010/02 /our-barriers-to-love-mondays-mindful-quote-with-rumi/.

15. Charlotte V. Witvliet, "Forgiveness and Health: Review and Reflections on a Matter of Faith, Feelings, and Physiology," *Journal of Psychology and Theology* 29, no. 3 (September 2001): 212–24, doi.org/10.1177/009164710102900303; Kathleen A. Lawler et al., "A Change of Heart: Cardiovascular Correlates of Forgiveness in Response to Interpersonal Conflict," *Journal of Behavioral Medicine* 26, no. 5 (October 2003): 373–93; James W. Carson et al., "Forgiveness and Chronic Low Back Pain: A Preliminary Study Examining the Relationship of Forgiveness to Pain, Anger, and Psychological Distress," *Journal of Pain* 6, no. 2 (March 2005): 84–91, doi.org/10.1016/j.jpain.2004.10.012.

16. Jack Kornfield, *The Art of Forgiveness, Lovinkindness and Peace* (New York: Bantam Books, 2002), 48-51.

Chapter 8: Priming the Mind for Joy: Seven Practices

1. Gene Weingarten, "Pearls Before Breakfast: Can One of the Nation's Great Musicians Cut Through the Fog of a D.C. Rush Hour? Let's Find Out." *Washington Post*, April 8, 2007, washingtonpost.com /lifestyle/magazine/pearls-before-breakfast-can-one-of-the-nations -great-musicians-cut-through-the-fog-of-a-dc-rush-hour-lets-find -out/2014/09/23/8a6d46da-4331-11e4-b47c-f5889e061e5f_story.html.

2. Gene Weingarten, "Gene Weingarten: Setting the Record Straight on the Joshua Bell Experiment." *Washington Post*, October 14, 2014, washingtonpost.com/news/style/wp/2014/10/14 /gene-weingarten-setting-the-record-straight-on-the-joshua -bell-experiment/?noredirect=on&utm_term=.61842d229ab9; Gene Weingarten, "Chatological Humor: Monthly with Moron (September)," *Washington Post*, October 7, 2014, live.washingtonpost. com/chatological-humor-20140930.html.

3. Harris Poll, "Annual Happiness Index Again Finds One-Third of Americans Very Happy," April 20, 2018, theharrispoll.com /although-one-of-the-simplest-emotions-happiness-can-be-hard-to -explain-the-harris-polls-annual-happiness-index-is-therefore-useful -as-it-uses-standard-and-timeless-questions-to-calculate-americans/.

4. Julia K. Boehm and Sonja Lyubomirsky, "Does Happiness Promote Career Success?" *Journal of Career Assessment* 16, no. 1 (2008): 101–16, doi.org/10.1177/1069072707308140.

5. Barbara De Angelis, *Soul Shifts: Transformative Wisdom for Creating a Life of Authentic Awakening, Emotional Freedom, and Practical Spirituality* (Carlsbad, CA: Hay House, 2016), 65.

6. Rick Hanson, *Hardwiring Happiness: The New Brain Science of Contentment, Calm, and Confidence* (New York: Harmony, 2013).

7. R. Hanson, E. Hutton-Thamm, M. Hagerty, and S. L. Shapiro, "Learning to Learn from Positive Experiences," *Journal of Positive Psychology*, in press.

8. Thich Nhat Hanh, *Peace Is Every Step: The Path of Mindfulness in Everyday Life* (New York: Bantam, 1992).

9. Ernest L. Abel and Michael L. Kruger, "Smile Intensity in Photographs Predicts Longevity," *Psychological Science* 21, no. 4 (April 2010): 542–44, doi.org/10.1177/0956797610363775.

10. Nicola Petrocchi and Alessandro Couyoumdjian, "The Impact of Gratitude on Depression and Anxiety: The Mediating Role of Criticizing, Attacking, and Reassuring the Self," *Self and Identity* 15, no. 2 (2015): 191–205, doi.org/10.1080 /15298868.2015.1095794; Michael E. McCullough, Robert A. Emmons, and Jo-Ann Tsang, "The Grateful Disposition: A Conceptual and Empirical Topography," *Journal of Personality and Social Psychology* 82, no. 1 (January 2002): 112–27, doi. org/10.1037/0022-3514.82.1.112.

11. Barbara L. Fredrickson et al., "What Good Are Positive Emotions in Crises? A Prospective Study of Resilience and Emotions Following the Terrorist Attacks on the United States on September 11, 2001," *Journal of Personality and Social Psychology* 84, no. 2 (March 2003): 365–76, doi.org/10.1037//0022-3514.84.2.365; Philip C. Watkins, Dean L. Grimm, and Russell Kolts, "Counting Your Blessings: Positive Memories among Grateful Persons," *Current Psychology* 23, no. 1 (March 2004): 52–67, doi.org/10.1007/s12144-004-1008-z.

12. Paul J. Mills et al., "The Role of Gratitude in Spiritual Well-Being in Asymptomatic Heart Failure Patients," *Spirituality in Clinical Practice* 2, no. 1 (2015): 5–17, doi.org/10.1037/scp0000050; Mei-Yee Ng and Wing-Sze Wong. "The Differential Effects of Gratitude and Sleep on Psychological Distress in Patients with Chronic Pain," *Journal of Health Psychology* 18, no. 2 (February 2013): 263–71, doi.org/10.1177/1359105312439733; Alex M. Wood et al., "Gratitude Influences Sleep through the Mechanism of Pre-Sleep Cognitions," *Journal of Psychosomatic Research* 66, no. 1 (February 2009): 43–48, doi.org/10.1016/j.jpsychores.2008.09.002.

13. Rollin McCraty et al., "The Effects of Emotions on Short-Term Power Spectrum Analysis of Heart Rate Variability," *American Journal of*

Cardiology 76, no. 14 (December 1995): 1089–93, doi.org/10.1016/S0002-9149(99)80309-9.

14. Nathaniel M. Lambert and Frank D. Fincham, "Expressing Gratitude to a Partner Leads to More Relationship Maintenance Behavior," *Emotion* 11, no. 1 (February 2011): 52–60, doi.org/10.1037/a0021557; Amie M. Gordon et al., "To Have and to Hold: Gratitude Promotes Relationship Maintenance in Intimate Bonds," *Journal of Personality and Social Psychology* 103, no. 2 (August 2012): 257–74, doi.org/10.1037/a0028723; Alex M. Wood et al., "The Role of Gratitude in the Development of Social Support, Stress, and Depression: Two Longitudinal Studies," *Journal Of Research in Personality* 42, no. 4 (August 2008): 854–71, doi.org/10.1016/j.jrp.2007.11.003.

15. Barbara L. Fredrickson, "Gratitude, Like Other Positive Emotions, Broadens and Builds," in *The Psychology of Gratitude*, ed. Robert A. Evans and Michael E. McCollough (New York: Oxford University Press, 2004), chapter 8.

16. Ariana Huffington, *Thrive: The Third Metric to Redefining Success and Creating a Life of Well-Being, Wisdom, and Wonder* (New York: Harmony, 2015).

17. Martin E. P. Seligman et al., "Positive Psychology Progress: Empirical Validation of Interventions," *American Psychologist* 60, no. 5 (July–August 2005): 410–21, doi.org/10.1037/0003-066X.60.5.410; Philip C. Watkins, Jens Uhder, and Stan Pichinevskiy, "Grateful Recounting Enhances Subjective Well-Being: The Importance of Grateful Processing," *Journal of Positive Psychology* 10, no. 2 (June 2014): 91–98, doi.org/10.1080/17439760.2014.927909; Alison Killen and Ann Macaskill, "Using a Gratitude Intervention to Enhance Well-Being in Older Adults," *Journal of Happiness Studies* 16, no. 4 (August 2015): 947–64, doi.org/10.1007/s10902-014-9542-3.

18. University of Notre Dame Science of Generosity initiative, "What Is Generosity?" accessed February 8, 2019, generosityresearch.nd.edu/more-about-the-initiative/what-is-generosity/.

19. Soyoung Q. Park et al., "A Neural Link between Generosity and Happiness," *Nature Communications* 8 (2017): 15964, doi.org/10.1038/ncomms15964.

20. Christian Smith and Hilary Davidson, *The Paradox of Generosity: Giving We Receive, Grasping We Lose* (New York: Oxford University Press, 2014).

21. Andy Kiersz, "Volunteering in America Is at Its Lowest Level in over a Decade," *Business Insider*, February 25, 2016, businessinsider.com/

bls-volunteering-chart-2016-2; Office for National Statistics, "Billion Pound Loss in Volunteering Effort," March 16, 2017, visual.ons.gov. uk/billion-pound-loss-in-volunteering-effort-in-the-last-3 -years/#footnote_3.

22. Robert Rosenthal and Lenore Jacobson, "Pygmalion in the Classroom," *Urban Review* 3, no. 1 (September 1968): 16–20; Annie Murphy Paul, "How to Use the 'Pygmalion' Effect," *Time*, April 1, 2013, ideas.time. com/2013/04/01 /how-to-use-the-pygmalion-effect/.

23. Tara Brach (founder of Insight Meditation Community in Washington, DC), in discussion with the author, Spirit Rock Meditation Center, 2014.

24. Jennifer E. Stellar et al., "Positive Affect and Markers of Inflammation: Discrete Positive Emotions Predict Lower Levels of Inflammatory Cytokines," *Emotion* 15, no. 2 (April 2015): 129–33, doi. org/10.1037/emo0000033.

25. Dacher Keltner, "Why Do We Feel Awe?" Greater Good magazine, May 10, 2016, greatergood.berkeley.edu/article/item/why_do_we _feel_awe; Sara Gottlieb, Dacher Keltner, and Tania Lombrozo, "Awe as a Scientific Emotion." *Cognitive Science* 42, no. 6 (August 2018): 2081–94, doi.org/10.1111/cogs.12648.

26. Paul K. Piff et al., "Awe, the Small Self, and Prosocial Behavior," *Journal of Personality and Social Psychology* 108, no. 6 (June 2015): 883–99, doi.org/10.1037/pspi0000018.

27. David R Hamilton, *The Five Side Effects of Kindness: This Book Will Make You Feel Better, Be Happier & Live Longer* (London: Hay House UK, 2017).

28. Barbara L. Fredrickson et al., "Open Hearts Build Lives: Positive Emotions, Induced Through Loving-Kindness Meditation, Build Consequential Personal Resources," *Journal of Personality and Social Psychology* 95, no. 5 (November 2008): 1045–62, doi.org/10.1037 /a0013262.

29. Cendri A. Hutcherson, Emma M. Seppala, and James J. Gross, "Loving-Kindness Meditation Increases Social Connectedness," *Emotion* 8, no. 5 (October 2008): 720–24 doi.org/10.1037 /a0013237; Dominique P. Lippelt, Bernhard Hommel, and Lorenza S. Colzato, "Focused Attention, Open Monitoring and Loving Kindness Meditation: Effects on Attention, Conflict Monitoring, and Creativity—A Review," *Frontiers in Psychology* 5 (2014): 1083, doi. org/10.3389/fpsyg.2014.01083.

30. Julieta Galante et al., "Loving-Kindness Meditation Effects on Well-Being and Altruism: A Mixed-Methods Online RCT," *Applied*

Psychology: Health And Well-Being 8, no. 3 (June 2016): 322–50, doi.org/10.1111/aphw.12074.

31. Sharon Salzberg, *Lovingkindness: The Revolutionary Art of Happiness* (Boston: Shambhala, 1995).

Chapter 9: Everyday Magic:
From Mindful Sex to Mindful Eating

1. Lori, A. Brotto et al., "Mindfulness-Based Sex Therapy Improves Genital-Subjective Arousal Concordance in Women With Sexual Desire/Arousal Difficulties," *Archives of Sexual Behavior* 45, no. 8 (November 2016): 1907–21, doi.org/10.1007/s10508-015-0689 -8; Alexander Khaddouma, Kristina Coop Gordon, and Jennifer Bolden, "Zen and the Art of Sex: Examining Associations among Mindfulness, Sexual Satisfaction, and Relationship Satisfaction in Dating Relationships," *Sexual and Relationship Therapy* 30, no.2 (April 2015), 268–85, doi.org/10.1080/14681994.2014.992408.

2. Lisa Dawn Hamilton, Alessandra H. Rellini, and Cindy M. Meston, "Cortisol, Sexual Arousal, and Affect in Response to Sexual Stimuli." *Journal of Sexual Medicine* 5, no. 9 (September 2008): 2111–18, doi.org/10.1111/j.1743-6109.2008.00922.x.

3. Tomás Cabeza de Baca et al., "Sexual Intimacy in Couples Is Associated with Longer Telomere Length," *Psychoneuroendocrinology* 81 (July 2017): 46–51, doi.org/10.1016/j.psyneuen.2017.03.022.

4. Marsha Lucas, "Stay-at-Om Sex: Bigger Is Better, but not Where You Think," *Psychology Today*, April 14, 2010, psychologytoday.com /us/blog/rewire-your-brain-love/201004 /stay-om-sex-bigger-is-better-not-where-you-think.

5. Jessica Graham, *Good Sex: Getting Off without Checking Out* (Berkeley: North Atlantic Books, 2017).

6. Barry Schwartz, *The Paradox of Choice: Why More Is Less* (New York: Harper Collins, 2004).

7. Schwartz, *The Paradox of Choice*.

8. Barry Schwartz et al., "Maximizing Versus Satisficing: Happiness Is a Matter of Choice." *Journal of Personality and Social Psychology* 83, no. 5 (November 2002): 1178–97, dx.doi. org/10.1037/0022-3514.83.5.1178.

9. Esther Perel. Conference: Women Teach Men. Ojai, CA. July, 2018. Presentation Title: "Women Teach Men."

10. Damasio, Antonio R. *Descartes Error: Emotion, Reason and the Human Brain*. London: Vintage, 2005.

11. Shauna L. Shapiro, Hooria Jazaieri, and Philippe R. Goldin, "Mindfulness-Based Stress Reduction Effects on Moral Reasoning and

Decision Making," *Journal of Positive Psychology* 7, no. 6 (November 2012): 504–15.

12. Thomas Merton, *The Way of Chuang Tzu*, 2nd ed. (New York: New Directions Books, 2010), 54.

13. Coquelicot Gilland, personal coach and originator of the Compassion Matrix System, in discussion with the author, April 2014.

14. Ruth Q Wolever et al., "Effective and Viable Mind-Body Stress Reduction in the Workplace: A Randomized Controlled Trial," *Journal of Occupational Health Psychology* 17, no. 2 (April 2012): 246–58, doi.org/10.1037/a0027278.

15. Beth Rieken et al., "How Mindfulness Can Help Engineers Solve Problems," *Harvard Business Review*, January 4, 2019, hbr .org/2019/01/how-mindfulness-can-help-engineers-solve-problems.

16. Jill Suttie, "Mindful Parenting May Keep Kids Out of Trouble," *Greater Good* magazine, June 7, 2016, greatergood.berkeley.edu /article/item/mindful_parenting_may_keep_kids_out_of_trouble.

17. John M. Darley and C. Daniel Batson, "'From Jerusalem to Jericho': A Study of Situational and Dispositional Variables in Helping Behavior," *Journal of Personality and Social Psychology* 27, no.1 (July 1973): 100–108, dx.doi.org/10.1037/h0034449.

Chapter 10: A More Connected and Compassionate World

1. Adam Lueke and Bryan Gibson, "Mindfulness Meditation Reduces Implicit Age and Race Bias: The Role of Reduced Automaticity of Responding," *Social Psychological and Personality Science* 6, no. 3 (April 2015): 284–91, doi.org/10.1177/1948550614559651.

2. Ruth King, *Mindful of Race: Transforming Racism from the Inside Out* (Boulder, CO: Sounds True, 2018), 73.

3. Derald Wing Sue and David Sue, *Counseling the Culturally Diverse: Theory and Practice*, 7th ed. (New Jersey: Wiley, 2015).

4. Maya Angelou, "Human Family," *I Shall Not Be Moved* (New York: Random House, 1990), 4–5.

5. "Genetics vs. Genomics Fact Sheet," National Human Genome Research Institute (NHGRI), last modified September 7, 2018, genome.gov/19016904/faq-about-genetic-and-genomic-science/.

6. Martin Luther King Jr., "Letter from Birmingham Jail," April 16, 1963, via University of Pennsylvania African Studies Center, accessed February 15, 2019, africa.upenn.edu/Articles_Gen /Letter_Birmingham.html.

7. John Muir, *My First Summer in the Sierra* (Boston: Houghton Mifflin,

1911), 110.

8. Albert Einstein to Norman Salit, March 4, 1950: Condolence Letter. Copyright@ Hebrew University of Jerusalem.

Chapter 11: "Good Morning, I Love You"

1. Hafiz, *The Subject Tonight is Love: 60 Wild and Sweet Poems of Hafiz*, trans. Daniel Ladinsky (New York, NY: Penguin Compass, 2003), 12.

Bibliography

Abel, Ernest L., and Michael L. Kruger. "Smile Intensity in Photographs Predicts Longevity." *Psychological Science* 21, no. 4 (April 2010): 542–44. doi.org/10.1177/0956797610363775.

Adams, Claire E., and Mark R. Leary. "Promoting Self-Compassionate Attitudes Toward Eating Among Restrictive and Guilty Eaters." *Journal of Social and Clinical Psychology* 26, no. 10 (October 2007): 1120–44. doi.org/10.1521/jscp.2007.26.10.1120.

American Psychological Association. "Multitasking: Switching Costs." March 20, 2006. apa.org/research/action/multitask.

Angelou, Maya. *I Shall Not Be Moved*. New York: Random House, 1990.

Bernhardt, Boris C., and Tania Singer. "The Neural Basis of Empathy." *Annual Review of Neuroscience* 35, no. 1 (July 2012): 1–23. doi.org/10.1146/annurev-neuro-062111-150536.

Blackburn, Elizabeth H., and Elissa Epel. *The Telomere Effect: a Revolutionary Approach to Living Younger, Healthier, Longer*. New York: Grand Central Publishing, 2018.

Blatt, Sidney J., Joseph P. D'Affitti, and Donald M. Quinlan. "Experiences of Depression in Normal Young Adults." *Journal of Abnormal Psychology* 85, no. 4 (August 1976): 383–89. doi.org/10.1037/0021-843X.85.4.383.

Boehm, Julia K., and Sonja Lyubomirsky. "Does Happiness Promote Career Success?" *Journal of Career Assessment* 16, no. 1 (2008): 101–16. doi.org/10.1177/1069072707308140.

Bohn, Roger, and James Short. "Measuring Consumer Information." *International Journal Of Communication* 6 (2012): 980–1000. ijoc.org/index.php/ijoc/article/viewFile/1566/743.

Bowlin, Stephanie L., and Ruth A. Baer. "Relationships Between Mindfulness, Self-Control, and Psychological Functioning." *Personality And Individual Differences* 52, no. 3 (February 2012): 411–15. doi.org/10.1016/j.paid.2011.10.050.

Brach, Tara. *Radical Acceptance: Embracing Your Life with the Heart of a Buddha*. New York: Bantam, 2004.

Breathnach, Sarah Ban. *Simple Abundance: A Daybook of Comfort and Joy*. New York: Grand Central Publishing, 2009.

Breines, Juliana G., and Serena Chen. "Self-Compassion Increases Self-Improvement Motivation." *Personality and Social Psychology Bulletin* 38, no. 9 (2012): 1133–43. doi.org/10.1177/0146167212445599.

Brewer, Judson. "Mindfulness Training for Addictions: Has Neuroscience Revealed a Brain Hack by Which Awareness Subverts the Addictive Process?" *Current Opinion in Psychology* 28 (August 2019): 198–203. doi.org/10.1016/j.copsyc.2019.01.014.

Brewer, Judson A., Jake H. Davis, and Joseph Goldstein. "Why Is It So Hard to Pay Attention, or Is It? Mindfulness, the Factors of Awakening and Reward-Based Learning." *Mindfulness* 4, no. 1 (March 2013): 75–80. doi.org/10.1007/s12671-012-0164-8.

Brickman, Philip, Dan Coates, and Ronnie Janoff-Bulman. "Lottery winners and accident victims: Is happiness relative?" *Journal of Personality and Social Psychology* 36, no. 8 (August 1978): 917–27. doi.org/10.1037/0022-3514.36.8.917.

Brotto, Lori A., Meredith L. Chivers, Roanne D. Millman, and Arianne Albert. "Mindfulness-Based Sex Therapy Improves Genital-Subjective Arousal Concordance in Women With Sexual Desire/Arousal Difficulties." *Archives of Sexual Behavior* 45, no. 8 (November 2016): 1907–21. doi.org/10.1007 /s10508-015-0689-8.

Brown, Brené. *I Thought It Was Just Me (But It Isn't): Women Reclaiming Power and Courage in a Culture of Shame*. New York: Gotham, 2007.

Brown, Brené. *The Gifts of Imperfection: Let Go of Who You Think You're Supposed to Be and Embrace Who You Are*.

Cabeza de Baca, Tomás, Elissa S. Epel, Theodore F. Robles, Michael Coccia, Amanda Gilbert, Eli Puterman, and Aric A. Prather. "Sexual Intimacy in Couples Is Associated with Longer Telomere Length." *Psychoneuroendocrinology* 81 (July 2017): 46–51. doi.org/10.1016 /j.psyneuen.2017.03.022.

Campos, Rui C., Avi Besser, and Sidney J. Blatt. "Recollections of Parental Rejection, Self-Criticism and Depression in Suicidality." *Archives of Suicide Research* 17, no. 1 (February 2013): 58–74. doi.org /10.1080/13811118.2013.748416.

Carlson, Kristine. *From Heartbreak to Wholeness: the Hero's Journey to Joy*. New York: St. Martin's Press, 2018.

Carson, James W., Francis J. Keefe, Veeraindar Goli, Anne Marie Fras, Thomas R. Lynch, Steven R. Thorp, and Jennifer L. Buechler. "Forgiveness and Chronic Low Back Pain: A Preliminary Study Examining the Relationship of Forgiveness to Pain, Anger, and Psychological Distress." *Journal of Pain* 6, no. 2 (March 2005): 84–91. doi.org/10.1016/j.jpain.2004.10.012.

Conley, Chip. *Wisdom at Work: The Making of a Modern Elder*. New York: Currency, 2018.

Creswell, J. David, Baldwin M. Way, Naomi I. Eisenberger, and Matthew D. Lieberman. "Neural Correlates of Dispositional Mindfulness During Affect Labeling." *Psychosomatic Medicine* 69, no. 6 (July–August 2007): 560–65. doi. org/10.1097/PSY.0b013e3180f6171f.

Dahm, Katherine A., Eric C. Meyer, Kristin D. Neff, Nathan A. Kimbrel, Suzy Bird Gulliver, and Sandra B. Morissette. "Mindfulness, Self-Compassion, Posttraumatic Stress Disorder Symptoms, and Functional Disability in U.S. Iraq and Afghanistan War Veterans." *Journal of Traumatic Stress* 28, no. 5 (October 2015): 460–64. doi.org/10.1002/jts.22045.

Darley, John M., and C. Daniel Batson. "'From Jerusalem to Jericho': A Study of Situational and Dispositional Variables in Helping Behavior." *Journal of*

Personality and Social Psychology 27, no. 1 (July 1973): 100–08.
doi.org/10.1037/h0034449.

Davidson, Richard J., Jon Kabat-Zinn, Jessica Schumacher, Melissa A. Rosenkranz,
Daniel Muller, Saki F. Santorelli, Ferris B. Urbanowski, Anne White
Harrington, Katherine A. Bonus, and John F. Sheridan. "Alterations in Brain
and Immune Function Produced by Mindfulness Meditation." *Psychosomatic
Medicine* 65, no. 4 (July–August 2003): 564–70.
doi.org/10.1097/01.PSY.0000077505.67574.E3.

De Angelis, Barbara. *Soul Shifts: Transformative Wisdom for Creating a Life of
Authentic Awakening, Emotional Freedom, and Practical Spirituality.* Carlsbad,
CA: Hay House, 2016.

Deikman, Arthur J. *The Observing Self: Mysticism and Psychotherapy.* Boston: Beacon
Press, 1982.

Deitch, Joseph. *Elevate: An Essential Guide to Life.* Austin, TX: Greenleaf Book
Group Press, 2018.

Deng, Yu-Qin, Song Li, and Yi-Yuan Tang. "The Relationship Between Wandering
Mind, Depression and Mindfulness." *Mindfulness* 5, no. 2 (April 2014):
124–28. doi.org/10.1007/s12671-012-0157-7.

Doty, James R. *Into the Magic Shop: a Neurosurgeon's Quest to Discover the Mysteries
of the Brain and the Secrets of the Heart.* New York: Avery, 2017.

Duckworth, Angela. *Grit: Why Passion and Resilience Are the Secrets to Success.*
London: Vermilion, 2017.

Eagleman, David. *Incognito: the Secret Lives of the Brain.* Edinburgh: Canongate,
2016.

Feiffer, Jules. "I Grew Up to Have My Father's Looks." 1976. Pen and ink on paper,
7.5 x 13.7" (19 x 34.8 cm). Via Artnet, accessed December 02, 2018. artnet.
com/artists/jules-feiffer/i-grew-up-to-have-my-fathers-looks
-osXdy07J8D04CdF44Fzx_A2.

Ferguson, Yuna L., and Kennon M. Sheldon. "Trying to Be Happier Really Can
Work: Two Experimental Studies." *Journal of Positive Psychology* 8, no. 1
(January 2013): 23–33. doi.org/10.1080/17439760.2012.747000.

Fjorback, Lone O., Mikkel Arendt, E. Ornbøl, Per Fink, and Harald Walach.
"Mindfulness-Based Stress Reduction and Mindfulness-Based Cognitive
Therapy: A Systematic Review of Randomized Controlled Trials." *Acta
Psychiatrica Scandinavica* 124, no. 2 (August 2011): 102–19.
doi.org/10.1111/j.1600-0447.2011.01704.x.

Fredrickson, Barbara L. "Gratitude, Like Other Positive Emotions, Broadens and
Builds." In *The Psychology of Gratitude*, edited by Robert A. Evans and Michael
E. McCollough, chapter 8. New York: Oxford University Press, 2004.

Fredrickson, Barbara L., Michael A. Cohn, Kimberly A. Coffey, Jolynn Pek, and
Sandra M. Finkel. "Open Hearts Build Lives: Positive Emotions, Induced
Through Loving-Kindness Meditation, Build Consequential Personal
Resources." *Journal of Personality and Social Psychology* 95, no. 5 (November
2008): 1045–62. doi.org/10.1037/a0013262.

Fredrickson, Barbara L., Michele M. Tugade, Christian E. Waugh, and Gregory R.
Larkin. "What Good are Positive Emotions in Crisis? A Prospective Study of
Resilience and Emotions Following the Terrorist Attacks on the United States

on September 11, 2001." *Journal of Personality and Social Psychology* 84, no. 2
(March 2003): 365–76. doi.org/10.1037//0022-3514.84.2.365.

Galante, Julieta, Marie-Jet Bekkers, Clive Mitchell, and John Gallacher. "Loving-
Kindness Meditation Effects on Well-Being and Altruism: A Mixed-Methods
Online RCT." *Applied Psychology: Health And Well Being* 8, no. 3 (June 2016):
322–50. doi.org/10.1111/aphw.12074.

Garland, Eric L., Adam W. Hanley, Phillipe R. Goldin, and James J. Gross. "Testing
the Mindfulness-to-Meaning Theory: Evidence for Mindful Positive Emotion
Regulation from a Reanalysis of Longitudinal Data." *PLOS ONE* 12, no. 12
(December 2017): E0187727. doi.org/10.1371/journal
.pone.0187727.

Gazzaley, Adam, and Larry D. Rosen. 2017. *The Distracted Mind: Ancient Brains in
a High-Tech World*. Cambridge, MA: MIT Press, 2017.

Germer, Christopher K., and Kristin D. Neff. "Self-Compassion in Clinical
Practice." *Journal of Clinical Psychology* 69, no. 8 (August 2013): 856–67. doi.
org/10.1002/jclp.22021.

Germer, Christopher K., Ronald D. Siegel, and Paul R. Fulton, eds. *Mindfulness and
Psychotherapy*. New York: Guilford Press, 2005.

Gilbert, Paul, and Chris Irons. "Focused Therapies and Compassionate Mind
Training for Shame and Self-Attacking." In *Compassion: Conceptualisations,
Research and Use in Psychotherapy*, edited by Paul Gilbert, 263–325. London:
Routledge, 2005.

Goldstein, Elisha. "Our Barriers to Love: Monday's Mindful Quote from Rumi."
PsychCentral.com. Last updated February 15, 2010. blogs.psychcentral.com
/mindfulness/2010/02
/our-barriers-to-love-mondays-mindful-quote-with-rumi/.

Goleman, Daniel. *Emotional Intelligence: Why It Can Matter More than IQ*.
London: Bloomsbury, 1996.

Goleman, Daniel. *Social Intelligence: The New Science of Human Relationships*.
London: Arrow Books, 2007.

Goleman, Daniel, and Richard J. Davidson. *Altered Traits: Science Reveals How
Meditation Changes Your Mind, Brain, and Body*. New York: Avery, 2018.

Gollwitzer, Peter M., and Paschal Sheeran. "Implementation Intentions and
Goal Achievement: A Meta-Analysis of Effects and Processes." *Advances in
Experimental Social Psychology* 38 (2006): 69–119. doi.org/10.1016
/S0065-2601(06)38002-1.

Gordon, Amie M., Emily A. Impett, Aleksandr Kogan, Christopher Oveis, and
Dacher Keltner. "To Have and to Hold: Gratitude Promotes Relationship
Maintenance in Intimate Bonds." *Journal of Personality and Social Psychology*
103, no. 2 (August 2012): 257–74. doi.org/10.1037/a0028723.

Gottlieb, Sara, Dacher Keltner, and Tania Lombrozo. "Awe as a Scientific Emotion."
Cognitive Science 42, no. 6 (August 2018): 2081–94.
doi.org/10.1111/cogs.12648.

Graham, Jessica. *Good Sex: Getting Off without Checking Out*. Berkeley: North
Atlantic Books, 2017.

Gross, James J. "Emotion Regulation: Affective, Cognitive, and Social

Consequences." *Psychophysiology* 39, no. 3 (May 2002): 281–91.
doi.org/10.1017/S0048577201393198.

Gruber, Matthias J., Bernard D. Gelman, and Charan Ranganath. "States of
Curiosity Modulate Hippocampus-Dependent Learning via the Dopaminergic
Circuit." *Neuron* 84, no. 2 (October 2014): 486–96.
doi.org/10.1016/j.neuron.2014.08.060.

Hafiz. *The Subject Tonight is Love: 60 Wild and Sweet Poems of Hafiz*, trans. Daniel
Ladinsky. New York, NY: Penguin Compass, 2003.

Harris Poll. "Annual Happiness Index Again Finds One-Third of Americans Very
Happy." April 20, 2018. theharrispoll.com
/although-one-of-the-simplest-emotions-happiness-can-be-hard-to-explain-
the-harris-polls-annual-happiness-index-is-therefore-useful-as-it-uses-standar-
d-and-timeless-questions-to-calculate-americans/.

Hamilton, David R. *The Five Side Effects of Kindness: This Book Will Make You Feel
Better, Be Happier & Live Longer*. London: Hay House UK, 2017.

Hamilton, Lisa Dawn, Alessandra H. Rellini, and Cindy M. Meston. "Cortisol,
Sexual Arousal, and Affect in Response to Sexual Stimuli." *Journal of Sexual
Medicine* 5, no. 9 (September 2008): 2111–18.
doi.org/10.1111/j.1743-6109.2008.00922.x.

Hanh, Thich Nhat. *Peace Is Every Step: The Path of Mindfulness in Everyday Life*.
New York: Bantam, 1992.

Hanson, Rick. *Buddha's Brain: The Practical Neuroscience of Happiness, Love, and
Wisdom*. Oakland: New Harbinger Publications, 2009.

Hanson, Rick. *Hardwiring Happiness: The New Brain Science of Contentment, Calm,
and Confidence*. New York: Harmony, 2013.

Hanson, Rick, and Forrest Hanson. *Resilient: How to Grow an Unshakable Core of
Calm, Strength, and Happiness*. New York: Harmony Books, 2018.

Hanson, R. Hutton-Thamm, E., Hagerty, M. and Shapiro, S. L. "Learning to Learn
from Positive Experiences." *Journal of Positive Psychology*, in press.

Henderson, Virginia P., Ann O. Massion, Lynn Clemow, Thomas G. Hurley,
Susan Druker, and James R. Hébert. "A Randomized Controlled Trial of
Mindfulness-Based Stress Reduction for Women with Early-Stage Breast
Cancer Receiving Radiotherapy." *Integrative Cancer Therapies* 12, no. 5
(January 2013): 404–13. doi.org/10.1177/1534735412473640.

Hiraoka, Regina, Eric C. Meyer, Nathan A. Kimbrel, Bryann B. DeBeer, Suzy
Bird Gulliver, and Sandra B. Morissette. "Self-Compassion as a Prospective
Predictor of PTSD Symptom Severity Among Trauma-Exposed U.S. Iraq and
Afghanistan War Veterans." *Journal of Traumatic Stress* 28, no. 2 (April 2015):
127–33. doi.org/10.1002/jts.21995.

Hölzel, Britta K., James Carmody, Mark Vangel, Christina Congleton, Sita M.
Yerramsetti, Tim Gard, and Sara W. Lazar. "Mindfulness Practice Leads
to Increases in Regional Brain Gray Matter Density." *Psychiatry Research-
Neuroimaging* 191, no. 1 (January 2011): 36–43. doi.org/10.1016
/j.pscychresns.2010.08.006.

Huffington, Arianna. *Thrive: The Third Metric to Redefining Success and Creating a
Life of Well-Being, Wisdom, and Wonder*. New York: Harmony, 2015.

Hutcherson, Cendri A., Emma M Seppala, and James J. Gross. "Loving-Kindness Meditation Increases Social Connectedness." *Emotion* 8, no. 5 (October 2008): 720–24. doi.org/10.1037/a0013237.

Jacobs, Tonya L., Elissa S. Epel, Jue Lin, Elizabeth H. Blackburn, Owen M. Wolkowitz, David A. Bridwell, Anthony P. Zanesco, et al. "Intensive Meditation Training, Immune Cell Telomerase Activity, and Psychological Mediators." *Psychoneuroendocrinology* 36, no. 5 (June 2011): 664–81. doi.org/10.1016/j.psyneuen.2010.09.010.

Johannsen, Maja, Maja O'Connor, Mia Skytte O'Toole, Anders Bonde Jensen, Inger Højris, and Robert Zachariae. "Efficacy of Mindfulness-Based Cognitive Therapy on Late Post-Treatment Pain in Women Treated for Primary Breast Cancer: A Randomized Controlled Trial." *Journal of Clinical Oncology* 34, no. 28 (October 2016): 3390–99. doi.org/10.1200 /JCO.2015.65.0770.

Kabat-Zinn, Jon. "An Outpatient Program in Behavioral Medicine for Chronic Pain Patients Based on the Practice of Mindfulness Meditation: Theoretical Considerations and Preliminary Results." *General Hospital Psychiatry* 4, no. 1 (April 1982): 33–47. doi.org/10.1016/0163-8343(82)90026-3.

Kabat-Zinn, Jon. *Full Catastrophe Living: Using the Wisdom of Your Body and Mind to Face Stress, Pain, and Illness*. New York: Delacorte Press, 1990.

Kabat-Zinn, Jon. *Wherever You Go, There You Are: Mindfulness Meditation in Everyday Life*. New York: Hyperion, 1994.

Kabat-Zinn, Jon, Elizabeth Wheeler, Timothy Light, Anne Skillings, Mark J. Scharf, Thomas G. Cropley, David Hosmer, and Jeffrey D. Bernhard. "Influence of a Mindfulness Meditation-Based Stress Reduction Intervention on Rates of Skin Clearing in Patients With Moderate to Severe Psoriasis Undergoing Photo Therapy (UVB) and Photochemotherapy (PUVA)." *Psychosomatic Medicine* 60, no. 5 (September 1998): 625–32. doi.org/10.1097/00006842-199809000-00020.

Kaliman, Perla, María Jesús Alvarez-López, Marta Cosín-Tomás, Melissa A Rosenkranz, Antoine Lutz, and Richard J. Davidson. "Rapid Changes in Histone Deacetylases and Inflammatory Gene Expression in Expert Meditators." *Psychoneuroendocrinology* 40 (February 2014): 96–107. doi.org/10.1016/j.psyneuen.2013.11.004.

Kang, Min Jeong, Ming Hsu, Ian M. Krajbich, George Loewenstein, Samuel M. McClure, Joseph Tao-yi Wang, and Colin F. Camerer. "The Wick in the Candle of Learning: Epistemic Curiosity Activates Reward Circuitry and Enhances Memory." *Psychological Science* 20, no. 8 (August 2009), 963–73. doi. org/10.1111/j.1467-9280.2009.02402.x.

Kashdan, Todd B., Melissa C. Stiksma, David J. Disabato, Patrick E. McKnight, John Bekier, Joel Kaji, and Rachel Lazarus. "The Five-Dimensional Curiosity Scale: Capturing the Bandwidth of Curiosity and Identifying Four Unique Subgroups of Curious People." *Journal of Research in Personality* 73 (April 2018): 130–49. doi.org/10.1016/j.jrp.2017.11.011.

Keltner, Dacher. *Born to Be Good: The Science of a Meaningful Life*. New York: W.W. Norton, 2009.

Keltner, Dacher. "Why Do We Feel Awe?" Greater Good magazine, May 10, 2016. greatergood.berkeley.edu/article/item/why_do_we_feel_awe.

Khaddouma, Alexander, Kristina Coop Gordon, and Jennifer Bolden. "Zen and the Art of Sex: Examining Associations among Mindfulness, Sexual Satisfaction, and Relationship Satisfaction in Dating Relationships." *Sexual and Relationship Therapy* 30, no. 2 (April 2015), 268–85. doi.org/10.1080/14681994.2014.992408.

Kiersz, Andy. "Volunteering in America Is at Its Lowest Level in over a Decade." Business Insider, February 25, 2016. businessinsider.com/bls-volunteering-chart-2016-2.

Killen, Alison, and Ann Macaskill. "Using a Gratitude Intervention to Enhance Well-Being in Older Adults." *Journal of Happiness Studies* 16, no. 4 (August 2015): 947–64. doi.org/10.1007/s10902-014-9542-3.

Killingsworth, Matthew A., and Daniel T. Gilbert. "A Wandering Mind Is an Unhappy Mind." *Science*, November 12, 2010. science.sciencemag.org/content/330/6006/932/tab-figures-data.

King, Martin Luther, Jr. "Letter from Birmingham Jail." April 16, 1963. Via University of Pennsylvania African Studies Center. Accessed February 15, 2019. africa.upenn.edu/Articles_Gen/Letter_Birmingham.html.

King, Ruth. *Mindful of Race: Transforming Racism from the Inside Out.* Boulder, CO: Sounds True, 2018.

Kornfield, Jack. *A Lamp in the Darkness.* Boulder, CO: Sounds True, 2014.

Kornfield, Jack. *A Path with Heart.* New York: Bantam Books, 1993.

Kornfield, Jack. *The Art of Forgiveness, Lovingkindness and Peace.* New York: Bantam Books, 2002.

Kornfield, Jack. "What Really Heals and Awakens: Highlights from Symposium 2018." Psychotherapy Networker, May/June 2018. psychotherapynetworker.org/magazine/article/1163/what-really-heals-and-awakens.

Kozlowski, Anna. "Mindful Mating: Exploring the Connection between Mindfulness and Relationship Satisfaction." *Sexual and Relationship Therapy* 28, no. 1–2 (2013): 92–104. doi.org/10.1080/14681994.2012.748889.

Lambert, Nathaniel M., and Frank D. Fincham. "Expressing Gratitude to a Partner Leads to More Relationship Maintenance Behavior." *Emotion* 11, no. 1 (February 2011): 52–60. doi.org/10.1037/a0021557.

Lawler, Kathleen A., Jarred W. Younger, Rachel L. Piferi, Eric Billington, Rebecca Jobe, Kim Edmondson, and Warren H. Jones. "A Change of Heart: Cardiovascular Correlates of Forgiveness in Response to Interpersonal Conflict." *Journal of Behavioral Medicine* 26, no. 5 (October 2003): 373–93.

Lazar, Sara W., Catherine Kerr, Rachel H. Wasserman, Jeremy R. Gray, Douglas N. Greve, Michael T. Treadway, Metta Mcgarvey, et al. "Meditation Experience Is Associated with Increased Cortical Thickness." *Neuroreport* 16, no. 17 (November 28, 2005): 1893–97. doi.org/10.1097/01.wnr.0000186598.66243.19.

Lebuda, Izabela, Darya L. Zabelina, and Maciej Karwowski. "Mind Full of Ideas: A Meta-Analysis of the Mindfulness-Creativity Link." *Personality And Individual Differences* 93 (April 2016): 22–26. doi.org/10.1016/j.paid.2015.09.040.

Lippelt, Dominique P., Bernhard Hommel, and Lorenza S. Colzato. "Focused Attention, Open Monitoring and Loving Kindness Meditation: Effects on Attention, Conflict Monitoring, and Creativity—A Review." *Frontiers in Psychology* 5 (2014): 1083. doi.org/10.3389/fpsyg.2014.01083.

Lucas, Marsha. "Stay-at-Om Sex: Bigger Is Better, but Not Where You Think." *Psychology Today*, April 14, 2010. psychologytoday.com/us/blog/rewire-your-brain-love/201004
/stay-om-sex-bigger-is-better-not-where-you-think.

Lueke, Adam, and Bryan Gibson. "Mindfulness Meditation Reduces Implicit Age and Race Bias: The Role of Reduced Automaticity of Responding." *Social Psychological and Personality Science* 6, no. 3 (April 2015): 284–91. doi.org/10.1177/1948550614559651.

Lutz, Antoine, Julie Brefczynski-Lewis, Tom Johnstone, and Richard J. Davidson. "Regulation of the Neural Circuitry of Emotion by Compassion Meditation: Effects of Meditative Expertise (Neural Effects of Compassion)." *PLOS ONE* 3, no. 3 (March 2008): E1897. doi.org/10.1371/journal.pone.0001897.

Lyubomirsky, Sonja. *The How of Happiness: A Practical Guide to Getting the Life You Want*. London: Piatkus, 2010.

Magee, Rhonda V. *The Inner Work of Racial Justice: Healing Ourselves and Transforming Our Communities through Mindfulness*. New York: TarcherPerigee, 2019.

Maguire, Eleanor A., David G. Gadian, Ingrid S. Johnsrude, Catriona D. Good, John Ashburner, Richard S. J. Frackowiak, and Christopher D. Frith. "Navigation-Related Structural Change in the Hippocampi of Taxi Drivers." *Proceedings of the National Academy of Sciences* 97, no. 8 (April 11, 2000): 4398–403. doi.org/10.1073/pnas.070039597.

Mark, Gloria, Daniela Gudith, and Ulrich Klocke. "The Cost of Interrupted Work: More Speed and Stress." *Proceedings of the SIGCHI Conference on Human Factors in Computing Systems* 2008, 107–10. ics.uci.edu/~gmark/chi08-mark.pdf.

Maté, Gabor. *In the Realm of Hungry Ghosts: Close Encounters with Addiction*. Toronto: Vintage Canada, 2012.

Matousek, Rose H., Patricia L. Dobkin, and Jens Pruessner. "Cortisol as a Marker for Improvement in Mindfulness-Based Stress Reduction." *Complementary Therapies in Clinical Practice* 16, no. 1 (February 2010): 13–19. doi.org/10.1016/j.ctcp.2009.06.004.

McCraty, Rollin, Mike Atkinson, William A. Tiller, Glen Rein, and Alan D. Watkins. "The Effects of Emotions on Short-Term Power Spectrum Analysis of Heart Rate Variability." *American Journal of Cardiology* 76, no. 14 (December 1995): 1089–93. doi.org/10.1016/S0002-9149(99)80309-9.

McCullough, Michael E., Robert A. Emmons, and Jo-Ann Tsang. "The Grateful Disposition: A Conceptual and Empirical Topography." *Journal of Personality and Social Psychology* 82, no. 1 (January 2002): 112–27, doi.org/10.1037/0022-3514.82.1.112.

Merton, Thomas. *The Way of Chuang Tzu*. 2nd ed. New York: New Directions Books, 2010.

Miller, John J., Ken Fletcher, and Jon Kabat-Zinn. "Three-Year Follow-Up and Clinical Implications of a Mindfulness Meditation-Based Stress Reduction Intervention in the Treatment of Anxiety Disorders." *General Hospital Psychiatry* 17, no. 3 (May 1995): 192–200, doi.org/10.1016/0163-8343(95)00025-M.

Mills, Paul J., Laura Redwine, Kathleen Wilson, Meredith A. Pung, Kelly Chinh, Barry H. Greenberg, Ottar Lunde, Alan Maisel, Ajit Raisinghani, Alex Wood, et al. "The Role of Gratitude in Spiritual Well-Being in Asymptomatic Heart Failure Patients." *Spirituality in Clinical Practice* 2, no. 1 (2015): 5–17. doi.org/10.1037/scp0000050.

Monti, Daniel A., Caroline Peterson, Elisabeth J. Shakin Kunkel, Walter W. Hauck, Edward Pequignot, Lora Rhodes, and George C. Brainard. "A Randomized, Controlled Trial of Mindfulness-Based Art Therapy (MBAT) for Women with Cancer." *Psycho-Oncology* 15, no. 5 (May 2006): 363–73. doi.org/10.1002/pon.988.

Mrazek, Michael D., Michael S. Franklin, Dawa Tarchin Phillips, Benjamin Baird, and Jonathan W. Schooler. "Mindfulness Training Improves Working Memory Capacity and GRE Performance While Reducing Mind Wandering." *Psychological Science* 24, no. 5 (May 2013): 776–81. doi.org/10.1177/0956797612459659.

Muir, John. *My First Summer in the Sierra*. Boston: Houghton Mifflin, 1911.

National Human Genome Research Institute (NHGRI). "Genetics vs. Genomics Fact Sheet." Last modified September 7, 2018. genome.gov/19016904/faq-about-genetic-and-genomic-science/.

Neff, Kristin. *Self-Compassion: The Proven Power of Being Kind to Yourself*. New York: William Morrow, 2011.

Neff, Kristin, and Christopher Germer. *The Mindful Self-Compassion Workbook: A Proven Way to Accept Yourself, Build Inner Strength, and Thrive*. New York: Guildford Press, 2018.

Neff, Kristin D., and S. Natasha Beretvas. *Self and Identity* 12, no. 1 (2013): 78–98. doi.org/10.1080/15298868.2011.639548.

Ng, Mei-Yee, and Wing-Sze Wong. "The Differential Effects of Gratitude and Sleep on Psychological Distress in Patients with Chronic Pain." *Journal of Health Psychology* 18, no. 2 (February 2013): 263–71. doi.org/10.1177/1359105312439733.

Niazi, Asfandyar Khan, and Shaharyar Khan Niazi. "Mindfulness-Based Stress Reduction: A Non-Pharmacological Approach for Chronic Illnesses." *North American Journal of Medical Sciences* 3, no. 1 (January 2011): 20–23. doi.org/10.4297/najms.2011.320.

Ochsner, Kevin N., Silvia A. Bunge, James J. Gross, and John D. E. Gabrieli. "Rethinking Feelings: An fMRI Study of the Cognitive Regulation of Emotion." *Journal of Cognitive Neuroscience* 14, no. 8 (November 2002): 1215–29. doi.org/10.1162/089892902760807212.

Office for National Statistics. "Billion Pound Loss in Volunteering Effort." March 16, 2017. visual.ons.gov.uk/billion-pound-loss-in-volunteering-effort-in-the-last-3-years/#footnote_3.

Ong, Jason C., Rachel Manber, Zindel Segal, Yinglin Xia, Shauna Shapiro, and James K. Wyatt. "A Randomized Controlled Trial of Mindfulness Meditation for Chronic Insomnia." *Sleep* 37, no. 9 (September 2014): 1553–63. doi.org/10.5665/sleep.4010.

Ong, Jason C., Shauna L. Shapiro, and Rachel Manber. "Combining Mindfulness Meditation with Cognitive-Behavior Therapy for Insomnia: A Treatment-Development Study." *Behavior Therapy* 39, no. 2 (June 2008): 171–82. doi.org/10.1016/j.beth.2007.07.002.

Ornish, Dean, and Anne Ornish. *Undo It! How Simple Lifestyle Changes Can Reverse Most Chronic Diseases*. New York: Ballantine Books, 2019.

Ortigue, Stephanie, Scott T. Grafton, and Francesco Bianchi-Demicheli. "Correlation between Insula Activation and Self-reported Quality of Orgasm in Women." *NeuroImage* 37, no. 2 (August 2007): 551–60. doi.org/10.1016/j.neuroimage.2007.05.026.

Ostafin, Brian D., and Kyle T. Kassman. "Stepping out of History: Mindfulness Improves Insight Problem Solving." *Consciousness and Cognition* 21, no. 2 (June 2012): 1031–36. doi.org/10.1016/j.concog.2012.02.014.

Ostaseski, Frank. *The Five Invitations: Discovering What Death Can Teach Us about Living Fully*. New York: Flatiron Books, 2019.

Park, Soyoung Q., Thorsten Kahnt, Azade Dogan, Sabrina Strang, Ernst Fehr, and Philippe N. Tobler. "A Neural Link between Generosity and Happiness." *Nature Communications* 8 (2017): 15964. doi.org/10.1038/ncomms15964.

Pascual-Leone, Alvaro, Dang Nguyet, Leonardo G. Cohen, Joaquim P. Brasil-Neto, Angel Cammarota, and Mark Hallett. "Modulation of Muscle Responses Evoked by Transcranial Magnetic Stimulation during the Acquisition of New Fine Motor Skills." *Journal of Neurophysiology* 74, no. 3 (September 1995): 1037–45. doi.org/10.1152/jn.1995.74.3.1037.

Paul, Annie Murphy. "How to Use the 'Pygmalion' Effect." *Time*, April 1, 2013. ideas.time.com/2013/04/01/how-to-use-the-pygmalion-effect.

Perel, Esther. *Mating in Captivity: Unlocking Erotic Intelligence*. New York: HarperCollins, 2017.

Petrocchi, Nicola, and Alessandro Couyoumdjian. "The Impact of Gratitude on Depression and Anxiety: The Mediating Role of Criticizing, Attacking, and Reassuring the Self." *Self and Identity* 15, no. 2 (2015): 191–205. doi.org/10.1080/15298868.2015.1095794.

Picard, Martin, Aric A. Prather, Eli Puterman, Alexanne Cuillerier, Michaeil Coccia, Kristin Aschbacher, Yan Burelle, and Elissa S. Epeil "A Mitochondrial Health Index Sensitive to Mood and Caregiving Stress." *Biological Psychiatry* 84, no. 1 (July 2018): 9–17. doi.org/10.1016 /j.biopsych.2018.01.012.

Piff, Paul K., Pia Dietze, Matthew Feinberg, Daniel M. Stancato, and Dacher Keltner. "Awe, the Small Self, and Prosocial Behavior." *Journal of Personality and Social Psychology* 108, no. 6 (June 2015): 883–99. doi.org/10.1037/pspi0000018.

Ricard, Matthieu, Antoine Lutz, and Richard J. Davidson. "Neuroscience Reveals the Secrets of Meditation's Benefits." *Scientific American*, November 2014, 38–45. scientificamerican.com/article /neuroscience-reveals-the-secrets-of-meditation-s-benefits/.

Rieken, Beth, Mark Schar, Shauna Shapiro, Shannon Katherine Gilmartin, and Sheri
    Sheppard. "Exploring the Relationship between Mindfulness and Innovation
    in Engineering Students." Paper presented at the American Society for
    Engineering Education Annual Conference, Columbus, OH, June 2017.
Rieken, Beth, Shauna Shapiro, Shannon Gilmartin, and Sheri D. Sheppard. "How
    Mindfulness Can Help Engineers Solve Problems." *Harvard Business Review*,
    January 04, 2019. hbr.org/2019/01
    /how-mindfulness-can-help-engineers-solve-problems.
Rigoni, Davide, Jelle Demanet, and Giuseppe Sartoni. "Happiness in Action:
    The Impact of Positive Effect on the Time of the Conscious Intent to Act."
    Frontiers in Psychology (2015). doi.org/10.3389/fpsyg.2015.01307.
Rizzolatti, Giacomo, Luciano Fadiga, Vittorio Gallese, and Leonardo Fogassi.
    "Premotor Cortex and the Recognition of Motor Actions." *Cognitive Brain
    Research* 3, no. 2 (April 1996): 131–41.
    doi.org/10.1016/0926-6410(95)00038-0.
Rockliff, Helen, Paul Gilbert, Kirsten McEwan, Stafford Lightman, and David
    Glover. "A Pilot Exploration of Heart Rate Variability and Salivary Cortisol
    Responses to Compassion-Focused Imagery." *Clinical Neuropsychiatry: Journal
    of Treatment Evaluation* 5, no. 3, (June 2008): 132–39.
Roeser, Robert W., Kimberly A. Schonert-Reichl, Amishi Jha, Margaret Cullen,
    Linda Wallace, Rona Wilensky, Eva Oberle, Kimberly Thomson, Cynthia
    Taylor, and Jessica Harrison. "Mindfulness Training and Reductions in Teacher
    Stress and Burnout: Results from Two Randomized, Waitlist-Control Field
    Trials." *Journal of Educational Psychology* 105, no. 3 (August 2013): 787-804.
    doi.org/10.1037/a0032093.
Rogers, Robert D., and Stephen Monsell. "The Costs of a Predictable Switch
    Between Simple Cognitive Tasks." *Journal of Experimental Psychology: General*
    124, no. 2 (June 1995): 207–231. doi.org/10.1037/0096-3445.124.2.207.
Romm, Joseph. *How to Go Viral and Reach Millions: Top Persuasion Secrets from
    Social Media Superstars, Jesus, Shakespeare, Oprah, and Even Donald Trump.*
    Eugene, OR: Luminare Press, 2018.
Rosenthal, Robert, and Lenore Jacobson. "Pygmalion in the Classroom." *Urban
    Review* 3, no. 1 (September 1968): 16–20.
Salzberg, Sharon. *Lovingkindness: The Revolutionary Art of Happiness.* Boston:
    Shambhala, 1995.
Sbarra, David A., Hillary L. Smith, and Matthias R. Mehl. "When Leaving Your Ex,
    Love Yourself: Observational Ratings of Self-Compassion Predict the Course
    of Emotional Recovery Following Marital Separation." *Psychological Science* 23,
    no. 3 (March 2012): 261–69.
    doi.org/10.1177/0956797611429466.
Schwartz, Barry. *The Paradox of Choice: Why More Is Less.* New York: Harper
    Collins, 2004.
Schwartz, Barry, Andrew Ward, John Monterosso, Sonja Lyubomirsky, Katherine
    White, and Darrin R. Lehman. "Maximizing Versus Satisficing: Happiness
    Is a Matter of Choice." *Journal of Personality and Social Psychology* 83, no. 5
    (November 2002): 1178-197. dx.doi.org/10.1037/0022-3514.83.5.1178.

Segal, Zindel V., J. Mark G. Williams, and John D. Teasdale. *Mindfulness-Based Cognitive Therapy for Depression.* 2nd ed. New York: The Guilford Press, 2018.

Seligman, Martin E. P., Tracy A. Steen, Nansook Park, and Christopher Peterson. (2005). "Positive Psychology Progress: Empirical Validation of Interventions." *American Psychologist* 60, no. 5 (July–Agust 2005): 410–421. doi. org/10.1037/0003-066X.60.5.410.

Shahar, Golan, Christopher C. Henrich, Annick Winokur, Sidney J. Blatt, Gabriel P. Kuperminc, and Bonnie J. Leadbeater. "Self-Criticism and Depressive Symptomatology Interact to Predict Middle School Academic Achievement." *Journal of Clinical Psychology* 62, no. 1 (January 2006): 147–55. doi. org/10.1002/jclp.20210.

Shapiro, Shauna L., Richard R. Bootzin, Aurelio J. Figueredo, Ana Maria Lopez, and Gary E. Schwartz. "The Efficacy of Mindfulness-Based Stress Reduction in the Treatment of Sleep Disturbance in Women with Breast Cancer: An Exploratory Study." *Journal of Psychosomatic Research* 54, no. 1 (January 2003): 85–91. doi.org/10.1016/S0022-3999(02)00546-9.

Shapiro, Shauna L., Linda E. Carlson, John A. Astin, and Benedict Freedman. "Mechanisms of Mindfulness." *Journal of Clinical Psychology* 62, no. 3 (March 2006): 373–86. doi.org/10.1002/jclp.20237.

Shapiro, Shauna L., Hooria Jazaieri, and Philippe R Goldin. "Mindfulness-Based Stress Reduction effects on Moral Reasoning and Decision Making." *Journal of Positive Psychology* 7, no. 6 (November 2012): 504–15.

Shapiro, Shauna L., Kristen E. Lyons, Richard C. Miller, Britta Butler, Cassandra Vieten, and Philip David Zelazo. "Contemplation in the Classroom: A New Direction for Improving Childhood Education." *Educational Psychology Review* 27, no. 1 (March 2015): 1–30. doi.org/10.1007/s10648-014-9265-3.

Shapiro, Shauna L., and Gary E. Schwartz. "The Role of Intention in Self-Regulation: Toward Intentional Systemic Mindfulness." In *Handbook of Self-Regulation*, edited by Monique Boekaerts, Paul R. Pintrich, and Moshe Zeidner, 253–73. New York: Academic Press, 1999. doi.org/10.1016 /B978-012109890-2/50037-8.

Shapiro, Shauna L., Gary E. Schwartz, and Ginny Bonner. "Effects of Mindfulness-Based Stress Reduction on Medical and Premedical Students." *Journal of Behavioral Medicine* 21, no. 6 (December 1998): 581–99. doi.org/10.1023/A:1018700829825.

Shapiro, Shauna L., David E. Shapiro, and Gary E. R. Schwartz. "Stress Management in Medical Education: A Review of the Literature." *Academic Medicine* 75, no. 7 (July 2000): 748–59.

Shelton, Alan. *Life Beyond Burnout: Recovering Joy in Your Work.* Carlsbad, CA: Balboa Press, 2018.

Siegel, Daniel J. *Aware: The Science and Practice of Presence — The Groundbreaking Meditation Practice.* New York: TarcherPerigee, 2018.

Siegel, Daniel J. "Mindful Awareness, Mindsight, and Neural Integration." *The Humanistic Psychologist* 37, no. 2 (April–June 2009): 137–58. doi.org/10.1080/08873260902892220.

Siegel, Daniel J. "Mindfulness Training and Neural Integration: Differentiation of Distinct Streams of Awareness and the Cultivation of Well-Being." *Social*

Cognitive and Affective Neuroscience 2, no. 4 (December 2007): 259–63. doi.org/10.1093/scan/nsm034.

Siegel, Daniel J. *Mindsight: The New Science of Personal Transformation.* Carlton North, Vic.: Scribe Publications, 2009.

Siegel, Daniel J. *The Developing Mind, Second Edition: How Relationships and the Brain Interact to Shape Who We Are.* New York: Guilford Press, 2012.

Simon, Herbert A. "Designing Organizations for an Information-Rich World." In *Computers, Communication, and the Public Interest,* edited by Martin Greenberger, 40–41. Baltimore, MD: Johns Hopkins Press, 1971.

Smith, Christian, and Hilary Davidson. *The Paradox of Generosity: Giving We Receive, Grasping We Lose.* New York: Oxford University Press, 2014.

Stellar, Jennifer E., Neha John-Henderson, Craig L. Anderson, Amie M. Gordon, Galen D. McNeil, Dacher Keltner. "Positive Affect and Markers of Inflammation: Discrete Positive Emotions Predict Lower Levels of Inflammatory Cytokines." *Emotion* 15, no. 2 (April 2015): 129–33. doi.org/10.1037/emo0000033.

Sue, Derald Wing, and David Sue. *Counseling the Culturally Diverse: Theory and Practice.* 7th ed. New Jersey: Wiley, 2015.

Suttie, Jill. "Mindful Parenting May Keep Kids Out of Trouble." *Greater Good* magazine, June 7, 2016. greatergood.berkeley.edu/article/item/mindful_parenting_may_keep_kids_out_of_trouble.

Tang, Yi-Yuan., Yinghua Ma, Junhong Wang, Yaxin Fan, Shigang Feng, Qilin Lu, Qingbao Yu, Danni Sui, Mary K. Rothbart, Ming Fan, et al. "Short-Term Meditation Training Improves Attention and Self-Regulation." *Proceedings of the National Academy of Sciences* 104, no. 43 (November 2007), 17152–56. doi.org/10.1073/pnas.0707678104.

Tillich, Paul. *Love, Power, and Justice: Ontological Analyses and Ethical Applications.* New York: Oxford University Press, 1960.

Toole, Aubrey M., and Linda W. Craighead. "Brief Self-Compassion Meditation Training for Body Image Distress in Young Adult Women." *Body Image* 19 (December 2016): 104–12. doi.org/10.1016/j.bodyim.2016.09.001.

Uncapher, Melina R., and Anthony D. Wagner. "Minds and Brains of Media Multitaskers: Current Findings and Future Directions." *Proceedings of the National Academy of Sciences* 115, no. 40 (October 2018): 9889–96. doi.org/10.1073/pnas.1611612115.

University of Notre Dame Science of Generosity Initiative. "What is Generosity?" Accessed February 8, 2019. generosityresearch.nd.edu/more-about-the-initiative/what-is-generosity/.

Watkins, Philip, C. Dean L. Grimm, and Russell Kolts. "Counting Your Blessings: Positive Memories among Grateful Persons." *Current Psychology* 23, no. 1 (March 2004): 52–67. doi.org/10.1007/s12144-004-1008-z.

Watkins, Philip C., Jens Uhder, and Stan Pichinevskiy. "Grateful Recounting Enhances Subjective Well-Being: The Importance of Grateful Processing." *Journal of Positive Psychology* 10, no. 2 (June 2014): 91–98. doi.org/10.1080/17439760.2014.927909.

Weil, Andrew. *Spontaneous Happiness: A New Path to Emotional Well-Being.* New York: Little, Brown, 2013.

Weingarten, Gene. "Chatological Humor: Monthly with Moron (September)."
   Washington Post, October 7, 2014. live.washingtonpost.com/chatological
   -humor-20140930.html.

Weingarten, Gene. "Gene Weingarten: Setting the Record Straight on the Joshua
   Bell Experiment." *Washington Post*, October 14, 2014. washingtonpost.com
   /news/style/wp/2014/10/14/gene-weingarten-setting-the-record-straight-on
   -the-joshua-bell-experiment/?noredirect=on&utm_term=.61842d229ab9.

Weingarten, Gene. "Pearls Before Breakfast: Can One of the Nation's Great
   Musicians Cut Through the Fog of a D.C. Rush Hour? Let's Find Out."
   Washington Post, April 8, 2007. washingtonpost.com/lifestyle/magazine
   /pearls-before-breakfast-can-one-of-the-nations-great-musicians-cut-through
   -the-fog-of-a-dc-rush-hour-lets-find-out/2014/09/23/8a6d46da-4331-11e4
   -b47c-f5889e061e5f_story.html.

Wilber, Ken. *A Brief History of Everything*. Anniversary edition. Boulder, CO:
   Shambhala, 2017.

Witvliet, Charlotte V. "Forgiveness and Health: Review and Reflections on a Matter
   of Faith, Feelings, and Physiology." *Journal of Psychology and Theology* 29, no. 3
   (September 2001): 212–24.
   doi.org/10.1177/009164710102900303.

Wolever, Ruth Q., Kyra J. Bobinet, Kelley McCabe, Elizabeth R. Mackenzie, Erin
   M. Fekete, Catherine A. Kusnick, and Michael J. Baime. "Effective and Viable
   Mind-Body Stress Reduction in the Workplace: A Randomized Controlled
   Trial." *Journal of Occupational Health Psychology* 17, no. 2 (April 2012): 246-58.
   doi.org/10.1037/a0027278.

Wood, Alex M., Stephen Joseph, Joanna Lloyd, and Samuel Atkins. "Gratitude
   Influences Sleep through the Mechanism of Pre-Sleep Cognitions." *Journal of
   Psychosomatic Research* 66, no. 1 (February 2009): 43–48. doi.org/10.1016
   /j.jpsychores.2008.09.002.

Wood, Alex M., John Maltby, Raphael Gillett, P. Alex Linley, and Stephen Joseph.
   "The Role of Gratitude in the Development of Social Support, Stress, and
   Depression: Two Longitudinal Studies." *Journal Of Research in Personality* 42,
   no. 4 (August 2008): 854–71. doi.org/10.1016/j.jrp.2007.11.003.

Young, Shinzen. *Natural Pain Relief: How to Soothe and Dissolve Physical Pain with
   Mindfulness*. Boulder, CO: Sounds True, 2011.

Zhang, Jia Wei, and Serena Chen. "Self-Compassion Promotes Personal
   Improvement from Regret Experiences via Acceptance." *Personality and Social
   Psychology Bulletin* 42, no. 2 (2016): 244–58.
   doi.org/10.1177/0146167215623271.

Index

Note: Italicized page numbers denote figures.

About the Author

Shauna Shapiro is a professor, author, and internationally recognized expert in mindfulness and compassion. Dr. Shapiro has coauthored two critically acclaimed books, which have been translated into 14 languages: *The Art and Science of Mindfulness* and *Mindful Discipline*. She has published over 150 journal articles as well. She has been an invited speaker for the King of Thailand, the Danish government, Bhutan's Gross National Happiness Summit, the Canadian government, and the World Council for Psychotherapy, as well as for Fortune 100 companies including Google, Cisco Systems, Proctor & Gamble, and Genentech.

The *New York Times*, BBC, Mashable, the *Huffington Post*, *Wired*, *USA Today*, and the *Wall Street Journal* have all featured her work, and well over a million people have watched her 2017 TEDx talk "The Power of Mindfulness."

Dr. Shapiro is a *summa cum laude* graduate of Duke University and a fellow of the Mind and Life Institute, cofounded by the Dalai Lama. She lives in Mill Valley, California, with her son, Jackson, and can be found online at drshaunashapiro.com.

In loving memory of Beth Skelley,
book designer extraordinaire.
Her spirit lives on in our books and in our hearts.